D0202851

Imagining Virginia Woolf

Imagining Virginia Woolf

AN EXPERIMENT IN CRITICAL BIOGRAPHY

Maria DiBattista

PRINCETON UNIVERSITY PRESS
Princeton and Oxford

For Suzanne Nash

Contents

Acknowledgments

This is a book that chronicles the adventures of reading, but those adventures would never have been as rewarding and as entertaining as they were without the friends who shared their thoughts, advice, and lovable selves with me. Even when they have not directly commented on this work, I could not have written a word without benefit of the friendship and conversation of David Bromwich, Sam Hynes, Martin Karlow, Alfred and Barbara Mac-Adam, Ed Mendelson, Deborah Nord, Brigitte Peucker and Paul Fry, David Quint, Barbara Rietveld, and P. Adams Sitney. They have helped shape and enrich my life as a reader. Also invaluable in this regard have been Cynthia Avila, Julia Ballerini, Robert Caserio, Alan Dale, Lauren Davis, Jay Dickson, Ann Gaylin, Allan Hepburn, Marie-Paule Laden, Lee Mitchell, Barry McCrea, Lucy McDiarmid, Gaetana Marrone Puglia, Susan Nanus, Esther Schor, and Susan Wolf. Woolf is the reason I came to know and value the company as well as scholarship of Julia Briggs, Mia Carter, Christine Froula, Mark Hussey, Maria Cândida Smith, and Natalya Reinhold.

In the last several years, I have been fortunate enough to work with Sanja Bahunic, Masha Mimran, Rebecca Rainof, Erwin Rosinberg, Jacqueline Shin, Keri Walsh, and Emily Wittman, all talented young scholars at work on projects that have deepened my sense of Woolf's achievement. I am particularly grateful to Hermione Lee for the example of her critical and biographical writings and for her generosity as a reader and encourager of this work. I also owe special thanks to Brenda Silver, who read the manuscript attentively and sympathetically yet never hesitated to correct or supplement what I had written with more accurate or fuller representations of Woolf's literary personality. Hanne Winarksy provided all the moral as well as editorial support any writer could wish for and, that given, seemed ready to offer more.

My sister, Dina, never failed to find time—and room!—for me when I most needed to be in a place and among family that I love. As always, my sons, Daniel and Matthew, are at the heart of everything I write. Finally, I dedicate this book to Suzanne Nash, a careful and unfailingly imaginative reader who also just happens to be the most devoted and dearest of friends.

The Demon of Reading

1

How many departments a person has: needing historians,
psychologists, poets &c. to interpret.

—V. Woolf, "Notes for Reading at Random"

The Figment of the Author

How should one read a book? Virginia Woolf first asked this question nearly a century ago, but the years have, if anything, made the question more, not less urgent. Books about how to read (a poem, a novel) periodically appear, as do books—*How Proust Can Change Your Life, Reading Lolita in Tehran, The Little Chinese Seamstress*—chronicling the emotional and political benefits of reading. There are even books, like Pierre Bayard's *How to Talk about Books You Haven't Read,* that suggest how *not* to read a book and still get some benefit from it. Finally there are books that promise that *anyone* can become a reader, even the Queen of England, as happens in Alan Bennett's droll fantasy, *The Uncommon Reader,* in which Her Majesty, to the surprise of her subjects and the chagrin of her retinue, develops a late-life passion for reading so voracious and ardent that Charles Dickens, Thomas Hardy, Marcel Proust, Nancy Mitford, and Jean Genet are devoured with equal and unmitigated pleasure.

These books, whatever their individual merits and degrees of seriousness, and whether or not we actually consult them, serve as important reminders of how valuable, and yet fragile, a human art reading continues to be. That reading enhances life is the recurring theme of these works, a view I share but do not directly comment upon in this book. Instead I concern myself with a slightly different and probably less creditable question, one less frequently asked but perhaps of more personal interest to us as readers, namely, how one should read an *author?* This question is generally raised, if at all, in literary biographies. Asking it here in a work of literary criticism may strike some readers as impertinent. After all, reading has its protocols like any other form of human encounter. One of the fundamental rules we are taught to observe in reading imaginative literature is not to treat the author like a character in his or her own work. We are instructed (often scolded) to respect the difference between an author and a narrator and not to mistake the person who speaks to us in an essay for the much less accountable person hunched over the page—or, now more likely, over the keyboard—who is wrestling with all the fiends who bedevil the makers of sentences.

Still, no matter how sophisticated we may be in separating the narrative or essayistic "I" from the author, we often find that our reading becomes so intense that this distinction becomes increasingly unimportant, a finery only pedants would insist we adhere to. We want, even yearn, to know who the author is and what he or she thinks about things. "What interests the reader," writes Señor C, the writer impersonated by J. M. Coetzee in *Diary of a Bad Year,* is the quality of the author's "opinions themselves—their variety, their power to startle, the ways in which they match or do not match the reputations of their authors."[1] Even otherwise disciplined academic critics routinely disregard such principled separation of author and writerly persona in fashioning adjectives out of proper nouns in order to designate a certain authorial "style" or way of looking at the world. Hence the untroubled, indeed often knowing and confident, way critics as well as common readers are inclined to invoke "signature styles": heroic humanity is Homeric or Shakespearean; a lyric feeling is Miltonic or Wordsworthian; social canvasses are Balzacian or Dickensian; unfailing artistic intelligence is Flaubertian or Jamesian; psychological nightmares are Dostoevskian or Conradian; modern epics are Tolstoyan or Joycean. These coinages signal that we have identified something quintessential about a writer's style or manner of interpreting and representing experience. To describe a style as Faulknerian or Beckettian or Nabokovian, to take other and equally apposite examples, conjures up a host of literary moods, dispositions, and temperaments that coalesce to form an imprint as distinctive as a genetic code. This imprint, a trace-code of the authorial DNA, is our primary way of distinguishing the focused person who writes from that "bundle of accidents and incoherence that sits down at breakfast,"[2] as Yeats somewhat comically described the writer of prose.

Yet however expert we become in deciphering the authorial code, we can never know the person who writes *directly* through her writing. This is an odder claim than it may initially appear, when you consider that the writer may divulge the most intimate secrets of her inner life through the very things she chooses to write about and by the way she writes about them. I want to make an even odder claim and insist that the person who writes never appears to us except as a figment of our imagination. This is what I mean by my title, "imagining" Virginia Woolf. I don't mean by this that I am making her up or attributing qualities to her that she may not indeed possess. Quite the opposite. It is Woolf who makes things up, who makes *herself* up—that is what it means, at a very fundamental level, to have an imagination and to use it in your writing. What I fabricate is an image of her that has slowly formed in my mind—a figment I call it—from the impressions, some more concrete than others, that I collect as I am reading her. This figment of the author may coexist with, but should never be mistaken for, the "figure of the author." I suspect it matters little to most readers whether the author as a literary *figure* is dead or alive or temporarily missing in action. On the other hand, the figment, being a subjective creation and not a rhetorical or literary personification, has a different reality and possesses a different importance in the mind of the reader. The figment of the author that attends us in our reading tends to be evanescent, is often misconceived, but is never insubstantial in its impact upon us.

It was Woolf who alerted me to the inevitability of these figments and of their power to shadow and ultimately affect our intellectual and emotional relation to what we are reading. The first concrete piece of advice she gives the reader in "How Should One Read a Book?" is to try to become the author, but then, in a reversal that becomes more and more typical of her as she becomes so confident in her own opinions that she can afford to qualify and, when necessary, disregard them, she admits her inability to follow her own advice:

> We may stress the value of sympathy; we may try to sink our own identity as we read. But we know that we cannot sympathise wholly or immerse ourselves wholly; there is always a demon in us who whispers, "I hate, I love," and we

cannot silence him. Indeed, it is precisely because we hate and we love that our relation with the poets and novelists is so intimate that we find the presence of another person intolerable. And even if the results are abhorrent and our judgments are wrong, still our taste, the nerve of sensation that sends shocks through us, is our chief illuminant; we learn through feeling; we cannot suppress our own idiosyncrasy without impoverishing it.[3]

The demon who whispers to us, I hate and I love, is the guardian (or fallen) angel who prevents our total imaginative surrender to the spell of the author. Writing, we might say, is a spell worked by the figure of the author. The demon of reading works a counterenchantment, beguiling us with a *figment* of the author, a figment that originates in our own mind and whose existence is registered by the many excitations, some minimal, some thrilling in their force, that we feel along the "nerve of sensation" that is most exposed when we read.

Along this nerve, I suspect, pass those sensations that constitute what Roland Barthes identified—and heralded—as the pleasures of the text. Notable among the pleasures Barthes recommended (and seemed to enjoy) was "the amicable return of the author." Of course, Barthes was careful to explain that

the author who returns is not the one identified by our institutions (history and courses in literature, philosophy and church discourse); he is not even the biographical hero. The author who leaves his text and comes into our life has no unity; he is a mere plural of "charms," the site of a few tenuous details, the source of vivid novelistic glimmerings,

a discontinuous chant of amiabilities, in which we nevertheless read death more certainly than in the epic of fate; he is
not a (civil, moral) person, he is a body.[4]

I am interested, like Barthes, in the author who leaves his text and
comes into our life. I share Barthes's view that this author has no
unity but appears to us as a plural and often discontinuous being.
But I do not agree with Barthes's determination that the author
is not an imaginable person. The author who returns *is* more than
a body, if less than a civil, moral person. To put it somewhat
differently, the body of the author who comes into our life is a
figment with distinguishing features and characteristics that produce in our mind's eye that mirage called personality. The author
is a plural being, then, but her plurality is not exhausted by her
charms or amiabilities; it extends to her ability to imagine herself
not as a single person, but as many persons; not as one body, but
as anybody, somebody, even nobody (whose official and ennobled
form Woolf recognized under the name of Anon, the nameless
poet who sings our common lot).

What follows is an experiment in critical biography that takes
as its subject a literary personality, Virginia Woolf, who exists only
intermittently in the pages of her writing. Because it is a *critical*
biography, this book will not satisfy a reader who might be curious
about the kind of person Virginia Woolf really was. I do not talk
about her private feelings for her family or her friends or her ene-
mies, sift through details of her sexual life, such as it was, or speculate on the sources and nature of her periodic madness. Those
questions are addressed in traditional biography, of which Hermione Lee's *Virginia Woolf* is the most complete as well as compelling version we are likely to have.[5]

What a critical biography offers is something at once less and more personally satisfying—an attempt to portray the person captured in the writing itself. The first book on Woolf, written by her friend and admiring contemporary Winifred Holtby, presented itself as a "critical memoir."[6] Holtby could call on what she knew of Woolf as a living person in interpreting, as she did with great subtlety, the work that was then so fresh, at times puzzling, to contemporary audiences. However "intimate" my knowledge of Woolf may seem to me at any given moment, I have no objective personal knowledge of her to communicate.

Not a critical memoir, then, but a biography. And because it is a critical and not a conventional biography, it avoids the paradox that, as Terry Eagleton has noted, plagues traditional biography. As Eagleton explains the paradox, we read biographies

> to savor the shape and texture of an individual life, yet few
> literary forms are more predictable. Everyone has to be born
> and almost everyone has to be educated, oppressed by par-
> ents, plagued by siblings, and launched into the world; they
> then enter upon social and sexual relationships of their own,
> produce children and finally expire. The structure of biogra-
> phy is biology. For all its tribute to the individual spirit, it
> is our animal life than underpins it.[7]

The structure of a critical biography, on the other hand, is nonbiological; the author's imaginative personality, not her animal life, underpins it. The subject of this biography is not the historical person who was born in 1882 and died in 1941. The subject is Virginia Woolf, the figment who exists as much in the minds of her readers as in the pages of her books. Hers is a curious kind

of existence, one dependent on readers and critics with sufficient imagination to acknowledge she is there and sufficient curiosity to wonder what she is like. That wonder is increased when
we discover, which we shortly do, that a writer like Woolf possesses and communicates not a single, but a multiple personality.
I do not approach this multiple personality as a pathological con-
dition, that is, as a more public and controlled form of the
madness that periodically overwhelmed her. I take what many
may consider an even more perverse position: I treat her multiple
or plural personalities as the highest achievement of her disciplined art.

These various personalities take on life and definition as the
figment of the author that I—the reader—create in my own
mind. The figment of the author is conceived in the corners
of the mind where the demon of reading lurks, inviting us to
play with the feelings our reading has aroused. It is a form of
play Woolf would have approved, I am sure, since it was she
who taught me its rules, so different from the principles I was
officially taught in school. To encounter this figment, to describe
and trace the apparitions it takes in the mind, is the purpose of
this book.

I confess here that I did not at first realize that I was dealing
with a figment of my own making until, writing the essay that
now takes the title of "The Adventurer," I began to see connec-
tions between essays written for different occasions on ostensibly
different topics. Although each essay analyzed different aspects of
Woolf's writing, my remarks were determined less by a definite
critical "approach" or "method" than by Woolf's own literary
personality as it appeared to me at the time. In putting these essays together, I not only brought the figment, somewhat blurred

in individual pieces, into collective and high definition: I also came to face my own "demon" who, refusing to be silenced, plagues but also enriches my life as a reader. This demon has largely been ignored by academic criticism, but it still insists on being heard, no matter how impersonal or detached we think we are while reading.

The demon of reading is the demon in us who is interested not in universal truths, but in particular personalities. Aldous Huxley was one of the moderns who, like Woolf, detected and appreciated the presence of this demon. "People will cease to be interested in unknowable absolutes," he predicted,

> but they will never lose interest in their own personalities. True, that "personality as a whole," in whose interest the sexual impulse is to be restrained and turned into love, is strictly speaking, a mythological figure. Consisting, as we do, of a vast colony of souls—souls of individual cells, of organs, of groups of organs, hunger-souls, sex-souls, power souls, herd-souls, of those multifarious activities of which our consciousness (the Soul with a large S) is only very imperfectly and indirectly aware—we are not in position to know the real nature of our personality whole. The only thing we can do is to hazard a hypothesis to create a mythological figure, call it Human Personality, and hope that circumstances will not by destroying us, prove our imaginative guesswork too hopelessly wrong. But myth for myth, Human Personality is preferable to God. We do at least know something of Human Personality, whereas of God we know nothing and, knowing nothing, are at liberty to invent as freely as we like.[8]

Huxley and Woolf, writers of quite different talents, nevertheless share the modern view that we are not "in position to know the real nature of our personality whole." Getting to know our personality and the personality of others is compromised, Huxley implies, by our constitutional inability to be "in position" to look at ourselves and at others straight on. We see through a glass not only darkly, but obliquely, through the slanted perspectives of hate and love and all the various grades of feeling in between. We can never peer directly into our own consciousness and see ourselves as we really are; how much less can we know of the personality of others. Yet we have the option—Woolf might even call it the opportunity—to create out of what we do know of those "multifarious activities of our consciousness" a rather genial myth of Personality.

No one took better advantage of that liberty to invent Human Personality than Woolf herself. She projected herself into the characters of her novels. She developed a new kind of narrator—anonymous, without settled opinions, apparent prejudices, or any moral truths to convey, completely at ease in flitting in and out of the minds of her characters; a narrator unafraid to react—with laughter or with alarm, tenderness or mockery—to the way her characters behave; in short, a narrator who was willing to appear inconsistent, even perplexed in her effort to deal honestly with the feelings, however mixed or changeable or difficult, that Life, at any give moment, demands. She wrote essays and tracts in which she submerged her own voice in that of an assumed identity—Mary Beton, Mary Seton, Mary Carmichael in *A Room of One's Own*—to profess her most personal views about writing, sex, feminism, literature, and power.

This book identifies the most dominant of Woolf's various personalities and attempts to forge them into a Whole. This attempt at unification, inspired by the demon of reading, was, of course, doomed from the start. But, then, I was not in the position when I first began reading Woolf so many years ago to perceive, much less appreciate, the extent to which Woolf's writerly personality contained Multitudes. Even now, I can confidently identify and describe only five of them.

2

Personalities

For someone who believed that "the people whom we admire most as writers . . . have something elusive, enigmatic, impersonal about them,"[1] Virginia Woolf had decidedly strong feelings about the personalities of other writers. Not even ideological differences could dislodge her affections for writers once they were formed. Thus the woman who wrote so passionately about the inequities institutionalized and routinely inflicted by patriarchal society openly confessed her love for "a man who, if he had lived today, would have been the upholder of all the most detestable institutions of his country; but for all that a great writer." Then, in a gush of adoration, Woolf reveals the name of her idol: "no woman can read the life of this man and his diary and novels without being head over ears in love with Walter Scott."[2]

Manliness of a different sort could inspire an aversion equally intense. Her feelings for Byron were arguably the most intemperate: "Intolerably condescending, ineffably vain, a barber's block to look at, compound of bully and lap-dog, now hectoring, now swimming in vapours of sentimental twaddle, tedious, egotistical, melodramatic, the character of Byron," she insisted, "is the least attractive in the history of letters." "But no wonder," she then mischievously remarks, "that every man was in love with him. In their company he must have been irresistible; brilliant and courageous; dashing and satirical; downright and tremendous; the conqueror of women and the companion of heroes—everything that strong men believe themselves to be and weak men envy them for being."[3] She was just as finicky about the female company she imagined she might or might not enjoy. Although she admired Jane Austen, she would not especially relish finding herself alone in a room with her. "A sense of meaning withheld, a smile at something unseen, an atmosphere of perfect control and courtesy mixed with something finely satirical which, were it not directed against things in general rather than individuals, would," Woolf felt, "make it alarming to find her at home." She would much prefer spending time with Charlotte Brontë; she was convinced that such a woman "so easily stirred by timely mention of the Duke of Wellington, so vehement, irrational, and caustic, would be far easier to know, easier, it seems to me, to love."[4]

These last two admissions come in a little-remarked essay, "Personalities," in which Woolf rehearses one of the major principles of her art—that "the great passages in literature have about them something of the impersonality which belongs to our own emotions at their strongest." Yet even as she celebrates the "happy fate for literature" that we moderns have no, or at best a weak, *personal* sense of the Greek dramatists, she cannot help lamenting that "there is nothing in the way of anecdote to browse upon, nothing handy and personal to help oneself up by, nothing is left but the literature itself, cut off from us by time and language, unvulgarized by association, pure from contamination, but steep and isolated."[5] Nevertheless, Woolf suspected that to engage literature on such lofty ground, however commendable in principle, in practice entailed reading "with more ingenuity but with less humanity than the ordinary person." Presented with a literary work in its pristine state, uncontaminated by personal association or historic anecdote, the ordinary person, representing that segment of humanity Woolf, after Samuel Johnson, identified as the common reader, would feel the absence of something vital to the experience of reading itself. Woolf wonders whether that missing element might be "the character, the writer's personality, which we guess to be there, but which, save for glimpses, we can never find for ourselves?"[6]

Woolf proceeds not only to sanction, but actively to assist common readers in their guesswork, even though, affecting mock horror, she fears that in doing so, she exposes herself to charges of "critical malpractice." At first, her taking sides with the ordinary against the ingenious (i.e., professional and reputedly disinterested) reader seems in keeping with a stance she often takes in her reviews and critical essays, in which she frequently presents herself as a relatively uneducated or unprofessional critic, following her own likes and dislikes wherever they might lead her, undeterred by what others might say or think about the often indiscreet opinions she ventures. Still, it is one thing to be curious about the personality of the writer whose work we are reading, another to assign the very idea of a writerly personality such an important role in our own responses to literature. This concession flies in the face of Woolf's own cherished critical precepts, developed most cogently and with an equally confiding manner in *A Room of One's Own*. In that rather famous and indisputably important feminist tract, Woolf had faulted Charlotte Brontë for failing to subdue her sense of injury and indignation in telling the story of Jane Eyre. Brontë, she charged, "had left her story, to which her entire devotion was due, to attend to some personal grievance."[7] Such an intrusion of personal feeling violates the exacting standards of Woolf's aesthetic, which dictate that the writer's partialities and prejudices not be allowed to compromise, warp, or otherwise distort the "integrity" of the writer as a chronicler of life.[8] Brontë, she proposes, should have been more like Shakespeare, that superlative and inspiring example of the artist possessed of a mind so "incandescent" that "[a]ll desire to protest, to preach, to proclaim an injury, to pay off a score, to make the world the witness of some hardship or grievance was fired out of him and consumed."[9]

What is missing in this ardent tribute to Shakespeare's consummate artistry is any real interest in how Shakespeare, the man, might have struggled to fire out all sense of grievance or hardship. Joyce devoted the entire "Scylla and Charybdis" chapter in *Ulysses* to an imaginary biography of Shakespeare based on the theory that his personal hardships, professional rivalries, and, most decidedly, sexual grievances were not fired out of him and consumed, but projected into the passionate action and language of his poems and plays. Where Joyce's Stephen Dedalus ransacks Shakespeare's life (of which we know remarkably little) to explain the signature themes of his art,[10] Woolf is hardly tempted to imagine what it might be like to *know* Shakespeare or spend even an hour in his company. Yet these are precisely the kinds of thoughts that arise from her reading Charlotte Brontë, who, though she indulged her desire to proclaim an injury in *Jane Eyre*, would have been, Woolf feels sure, someone she could have loved. This is a sufficiently obvious, if not glaring contradiction, in Woolf's thinking about who writers are and how they work on our sympathy and imagination. Still, as contradictions go, it proves an amazingly fertile one.

That may be why Woolf, who was fully aware of the inconsistency, showed little interest in resolving or eliminating it. For example, she admits in "Personalities" that reading works of literature in the light of the personalities they exhibit may divert our attention from great artists to those of lesser caliber since, Woolf maintained, "it is the imperfect artists who never manage to say the whole thing in their books who wield the power of personality over us."[11] Having offered this opinion, Woolf immediately thinks the better of it. No sooner does she proclaim that the life and opinions of more perfect artists have "been distilled into their books" than the figure of Keats intrudes into her consciousness, unsettling her argument. Keats, who famously proclaimed that "the poet . . . has no character," becomes Woolf's most compelling example of "the kind of writer whose personality affects us." Not all readers, however, are affected in the same way. The more general and still fashionable opinion, one Woolf initially seems to share, is that "If ever there was a lovable human being, one whom one would wish to live with, walk with, go on foreign travels with, it was Keats." But there are also dissenting views, which in some ways are more useful to Woolf in making her point about artistic personalities. She begins "Personalities" by quoting A. R. Symonds's "highly unfashionable" opinion that "there is something in the personality of Keats, some sort of semi-physical aroma wafted from it,"[12] which Symonds personally found unendurable. While Woolf did not share this feeling, she could understand it without trying to refute it. In fact, she was capable of impious thoughts about Keats herself. In an earlier essay, somewhat sheep-ishly entitled "Indiscretions," Woolf had entertained a rather com-plicated view of Keats. "There, if ever, was a man," Woolf writes with a generous dash of irony,

> whom both sexes must unite to honour: towards whom the personal bias must incline all in the same direction. But there is a hitch; there is Fanny Brawne. She danced too much in Hampstead, Keats complained. The divine poet was a little sultanic in his behavior; after the manly fashion of his time apt to treat his adored both as angel and cocka-too. A jury of maidens would bring in a verdict in Fanny's favour.[13]

As this passage makes quite plain, Woolf's own personal bias was inclined against the sultanic male, no matter how divine his po-etry. She was forever calling attention to the "hitch" of sex over which even finer—and, of course, lesser—men than Keats have stumbled. In the court of sexual opinion, Woolf can be found reliably testifying on behalf of the badgered, harassed, and patron-ized of her own sex. Her judgments are so winning because they are usually delivered with a sense of humor that makes them seem more impartial than they in fact are.

In the face of such acknowledged partialities, Woolf is forced to conclude, not unhappily it turns out, that when it comes to writers, the presence or absence of personality is not a reliable index of artistic merit: "Some show themselves, others hide them-selves," she determines, "irrespective of their greatness."[14] Once she takes this noncommittal view, she never forsakes it. Pursuing this line of thought and feeling, she wonders openly whether "a disposition to like or dislike which works its way into the text and possibly falsified its meaning" is simply a factor we can neither deny nor eliminate in our considerations of what it means to read, *really* read. Woolf suggests as much in posing a question to her own readers that hovers between a suggestion and a challenge: "do we only read with all of our faculties when we seize this impression too?"[15]

I take this question to be a rhetorical one. Woolf is not so much asking us our opinion as stating her own. She is recommending a practice of reading that accommodates our half-formed, possibly false impressions of the writer's personality, however subversive such a practice might prove to the orthodoxies, past or current, that either make personality a nonissue or exalt or condemn the author as an ideological figure with morally impeccable or politically despicable opinions. I intend to follow Woolf's prescription as if she had offered it with herself in mind. Following Woolf's suggestion was not, I must confess, as easy a task as I initially thought it would be. It is one thing to form an impression of an author while reading, another to render one's impressions as they accrue and modify themselves over time. The writerly personality will sometimes appear in sharp outline, sometimes in blurred or indistinct contours, against the expanse of a lifetime of writing. This difficulty would seem to become particularly pronounced in the case of a writer like Woolf, who, as many of her commentators have noted, most recently and meticulously her biographer Hermione Lee, "had different ways of presenting her own identity."[16] *Orlando*, Woolf's most fanciful, but in many ways most edifying biography of a writer, returns insistently to this notion of the "great variety of selves" that any person, but especially a writer, may reveal in the course of a single day. Orlando, as his/her biog-

rapher relates with increasing exasperation, "was strangely com-
pounded of many humours—of melancholy, of indolence, of passion, of love of solitude, to say nothing, of all those contortions
and subtleties of temper which were indicated on the first page,
when he slashed at a dead nigger's head; cut it down; hung it
chivalrously out of his reach again and then betook himself to the
window-seat with a book."[17]

Such changeableness may enrich and enliven, but also trouble
our sense of the writer's personality. This double possibility is
acknowledged in Woolf's pronouncement that "[O]ne's self is the
greatest monster and miracle in the world."[18] Even for Woolf, who
showed a flair for hyperbole, this seems an extreme, even slightly
hysterical proposition. Should we credit it? Surely any plausible
account of human character would avoid using the sensationalist
language of monstrosity and miracle. At the very least, Woolf
should make mention of the innate dispositions, acquired habits,
and social conventions that generally cooperate to prevent us from
becoming either a monster or a miracle, both conditions potentially fatal to our human status. This histrionic claim is all the
more surprising given that it arrives at the conclusion of her otherwise measured, if greatly admiring, essay on Montaigne, the only
writer, Woolf felt, who had mastered the art of "talking of oneself,
following one's own vagaries, giving the whole map, weight, colour, and circumference of the soul in its confusion, its variety,
its imperfections."[19]

We might reasonably wonder whether it was not the larger-
than-life figure of Montaigne that inspired Woolf's exaggerated
rhetoric, but rather the stress she felt in trying to convey how
difficult and, of course, how virtually endless is the art of talking
of oneself (analysis interminable if there ever was one). Woolf's

greater, if more subtle, point in this essay is that however confused, volatile, various, even miraculous Montaigne's self may seem, his personality becomes, after sufficient acquaintance, visible, vivid, even dear to us. Erich Auerbach, echoing, if not directly alluding to, Woolf in his own essay on Montaigne in *Mimesis*, interrupts his critical analysis of a passage from the *Essays* to inform his readers that "I had been reading him for some time, and when I had finally acquired a certain familiarity with his manner, I thought I could hear him speak and see his gestures." This trick of thought he credits to Montaigne's ability "to write as though he were speaking."[20] Many readers, grown accustomed to Woolf's own literary manner, a manner very much on display in her essay on Montaigne, may admit to experiencing Woolf as a writer in a somewhat similar way. It is not just that her voice has now become familiar to us in all of its various registers and intonations—in the novels, in the essays, in the diaries, in the letters. It is that she, too, infused her writing with the art of talking, so that her writing voice, which often strikes us as something that is spoken, is something we seem to *hear* in her prose. Thus we pick up a novel like *To the Lighthouse* and feel as if we have arrived just in time to overhear a crucial exchange in an ongoing family debate: "Yes, of course, if it's fine tomorrow";[21] or we begin a tract like *A Room of One's Own* and immediately find ourselves addressed as an interested, if skeptical, party to an argument that will not proceed without us: "But you may say, we asked you to speak about women and fiction—what has that got to do with a room of one's own?"[22]

These moments, in which Woolf displays her rhetorical skill in making herself heard, offer us opportunities for getting to know her as a distinct personality. That she makes herself so available, indeed so vulnerable, to us at such moments is odder than may first appear. Given her identification with the tradition and art of Anon, the nameless artist, "sometimes man, sometimes woman . . . the common voice singing out of doors,"[23] it seems strange, even bewildering, that Woolf was so willing to express—and thus reveal—her personality. The desire to be *known* to her readers is surely a strong motive in her personalizing her voice to the extent that she does. But there are more forces at work in her willingness to expose herself, sometimes in highly unflattering light. One of the most irresistible was Woolf's own sense of herself as a modern. The ability to communicate *oneself* was, for her, a sign of a modernity she could neither escape nor forswear. Her extensive reading for "Reading," an essay written in the 1920s, had left her with the historic impression that "the art of speech came late to England." It was an impression gleaned primarily from the incomplete, awkward, or broken testimony left by her English forebears:

> These Fanshawes and Leghs, Verneys, Pastons, and Hutchinsons, all well endowed by birth and nature and leaving behind them such a treasure of inlaid wood and old furniture, things curiously made, and delicately figured, left with it a very broken message or one so stiff that the ink seems to have dried as it traced the words. Did they, then, enjoy these possessions in silence, or was the business of life transacted in a stately way to match these stiff polysyllables and branching periods? Or, like children on a Sunday, did they compose themselves and cease their chatter when they sat down to write what would pass from hand to hand, serve for winter gossip round a dozen firesides, and be laid up at length with other documents of importance in the dry room above the kitchen fireplace?[24]

She would later distill these impressions into a single phrase in the notebook she kept for an essay, the last she was to write as it turned out, on the birth of the reader: "the modern: . . . the growth of articulateness."[25]

Hence the wonder as well as the gratitude Woolf feels for that voluble and eccentric personage, Sir Thomas Browne, "one of the first of our writers to be definitely himself."[26] Woolf commends Browne's writing to us because it raises, in the most personable and engaging way, "the whole question, which is afterwards to become of such importance, of knowing one's author."[27] Knowing one's author came to include, as we might expect, coming to know how the author knows—and chooses to present— himself. Here, again, the eccentric Sir Thomas Browne was an inspiration. His self-presentation was, in Woolf's estimation, an unself-conscious performance, and all the more creditable and reliable for that. In reading him, Woolf marvels how

the littleness of egotism has not as yet attacked the health of his interest in himself. I am charitable, I am brave, I am averse from nothing, I am full of feeling for others, I am merciless upon myself, "For my conversation, it is like the sun's, with all men, and with a friendly aspect to good and bad"; I, I, I—how we have lost the secret of saying that![28]

Woolf's own preoccupation with herself, registered in the rather endearing, if sorely troubled, diary entry—"How I interest myself"[29]—should be read next to her admiration, verging on envy, for the ease with which Sir Thomas Browne could say "I, I, I."

How many of us, common readers and professional critics alike, have lost the secret of saying that!

Women, of course, never fully possessed the secret—that is one of the central discoveries of Woolf's investigation into the character and history of women's literature. The history of women's writing is the history of women struggling to find ways to say "I" without being burdened by crippling self-consciousness or reproached for immodesty. When Woolf urges women in *A Room of One's Own* to secure a room of their own and five hundred pounds a year, it is partly in the hope that they would then begin to say "I"—I think this, I feel that—without being harassed by the censors within or chided by disapproving (or alarmed) critics without. Regrettably, this strong hope is often drowned out by the uproar surrounding her more famous complaint in *A Room of One's Own* that a man's writing is often blighted by a "straight dark bar" shadowing the page, a "shadow shaped something like the letter 'I.' "[30] What is lost in the uproar occasioned by this remark is the note of lament in her condemnation. Once we hear that note, her complaint sounds somewhat differently. It sounds less like a protest against the first-person pronoun than against the verbal ground into which certain masculinist powers have implanted it like a territorial flag. We have come over the years to appreciate Woolf's creative conjunctions of the first-person plural that invoked neither a royal nor an editorial but a choric we. But we have overlooked her interest in finding a way to say "I" that will not be diminished by the littleness of egotism. This "I" has important things to testify to: this is the "I" who can observe, describe, judge, and actually take *pleasure* in itself, an "I" who enjoys its powers to create and re-create the world. Woolf's fascination with this "I" led her to explore the various registers of what we could call the nonegotistical sublime.

THE NONEGOTISTICAL SUBLIME

This phrase, however odd it might initially sound, has the distinct merit of associating Woolf with the tradition of Romantic self-hood to which she, in fact, belongs. It takes us back one more time to the figure of Keats, who famously proclaimed that the "poet has no identity—he is continually in for or filling some other body" and who even more memorably criticized and distanced himself from the "Wordsworthian or egotistical sublime."[31] Both the idiom and example of Keats are echoed in Woolf's declared determination to resist the incursions of "the damned egotistical self," which, she confided to her diary, "ruins Joyce and [Dorothy] Richardson in my mind."[32] Later, in a more public venue, Woolf virtually adopts the Keatsean idea of poetic non-identity in her "Letter to a Young Poet." Writing to John Lehmann, Woolf contends that the art of writing can be learned "much more drastically and effectively by imagining that one is not oneself but somebody different":

> How can you learn to write if you write only about one single person? To take the obvious example. Can you doubt that the reason why Shakespeare knew every sound and syllable in the language and could do precisely what he liked with grammar and syntax, was that Hamlet, Falstaff and Cleopatra rushed him into this knowledge; that the lords, officers, dependants, murderers and common soldiers of the

plays insisted that he should say exactly what they felt in the words expressing their feelings? It was they who taught him to write, not the begetter of the Sonnets.[33]

Put aside for a moment the question of whether or not this is, in fact, sound advice. Focus instead on how Woolf's description of Shakespeare's creative state seems unduly agitated. At times she appears perilously close to identifying the imagination working at full power with the frenzy associated with manic hallucinations: voices from imaginary beings "rush" the mind into knowledge and compel it to ventriloquize "exactly what they felt in the words expressing their feelings." We might become reasonably concerned if we encountered this account of a creative "high" in a letter written by a friend, published in the *Times*, or posted on the Internet. But because it is Shakespeare's mind that is being described and analyzed, we know that this capacity to listen— not to listen politely, mind you, but to be overwhelmed by the clamoring voices of one's own creations—is a sign of triumphant and ecstatic imaginative power. "You will do well," she advises her young poet, "to embark upon a long poem in which people as unlike yourself as possible talk at the tops of their voices." Here Woolf envisages sublimity in its most dramatic and operatic form, the form, that is, with which the Shakespearean imagination endows it. It is a sublimity experienced and achieved by allowing voices originating deep within oneself to declaim, shout, assert themselves as loudly and as emphatically as they can.

Yet Woolf was also aware that the poet and the writer of prose, such as herself, has a different relation to language and hence a different way of accommodating those inner voices soliciting her imaginative attention: "The poet gives us his essence, but prose takes the mould of the body and mind entire."[34] According to this definition, the poet communicates his innermost essence, a distillation of his solitary being. This is why Woolf can logically claim that it is not Shakespeare, the physical being with personal memories and feelings to communicate, who generates the language of dramatic poetry. Poetic language is the language of "essence," language drastically abstracted and removed from all the particular feelings (love, hate) and vagrant moods (ranging from ecstasy to despair) that make up the life of any given Monday or Tuesday.

The writer of prose, on the other hand, communicates a different *form* of sublimity. It is the sublimity available to and experienced by an "I" who is an embodied rather than an abstract being. The "mould" of the author that is crafted in the language of prose accommodates both the bodily ego, with its instincts, reflexes, and behaviors, and the sentient mind in its conscious and unconscious activities. The nonegotistical sublime is the supreme incarnation, we might say, of this writerly personality as it is expressed through the mould language makes of "the body and mind entire." This writing I, which has its own special way of experiencing reality, can be said to mediate between the Wordsworthian egotistical sublime and Keatsean negative capability in which the conscious, self-interested ego is temporarily suspended. If the ideal language of poetry is, for Woolf, the language of being, the language of prose is, inevitably, the language of personality, the language that says "I, I, I."

I realize that there is little in this account of the writerly personality that will satisfy the trained psychologist or professional philosopher or academic critic, each equipped with a specialized language and established method to analyze the creative mind. Each might be inclined to dismiss my account of the nonegotistical sublime as a hopelessly romantic myth. But as Huxley appreciated in evoking the Myth of a Whole Personality, because myths are fanciful does not make them useless or negligible. Recall that Huxley envisioned the personality as superintending "a vast colony of souls—souls of individual cells, of organs, of groups of organs, hunger-souls, sex-souls, power souls, herd-souls," of whom "our consciousness (the Soul with a large S) is only very imperfectly and indirectly aware." His conviction that "we are not in position to know the real nature of our personality whole" is supported, surprisingly enough, by one of the first modern social psychologists to explore the structure and nature of the human personality, Gordon Allport.

Allport's writings provide a less poetic understanding of the way the writerly personality can cohere around the various selves it either experiences directly or simply assumes or imagines must exist. Allport was very much interested in promoting psychology as a science of becoming, "for it is precisely here," he wrote, "that our ignorance and uncertainty are greatest." Writing in 1955, he remarked:

> Our methods, however well suited to the study of sensory processes, animal research, and pathology, are not fully adequate; and interpretations arising from the exclusive use of these methods are stultifying. Some theories of becoming are based largely upon the behavior of sick and anxious people or upon the antics of captive and desperate rats. Fewer theories have derived from the study of healthy human beings, those who strive not so much to preserve life as to make it worth living. Thus we find today many studies of

criminals, few of law-abiders; many of fear, few of courage; more on hostility than on affiliation; much on the blindness in man, little on his vision; much on his past, little on his outreaching into the future.[35]

I am not concerned with the truth-value of this claim today, nor in sorting through the disputes between Freudian and anti-Freudian, existentialist and behaviorist schools whose antithetical, contending views of the mind's workings have complicated and confused as much as they have deepened our modern conception of the personality. What I find appealing and useful in Allport's approach is his contention that the healthy personality exhibits an imaginative capacity for affiliation, projection, and vision that makes life worth living.

Allport argues that if we focus on becoming as an imaginative process, we invariably encounter what he calls "the dilemma of uniqueness." This is the dilemma that confronts us whenever we look at and find ourselves responding (I hate, I love) to an individual personality. In defining the nature and scope of this dilemma, Allport resorts to the analogy and rules of language. "Each person," he writes, "is an idiom unto himself, an apparent violation of the syntax of the species. An idiom develops in its own peculiar context, and this context must be understood in order to comprehend the idiom. Yet at the same time, idioms are not entirely lawless and arbitrary; indeed they can be known for what they are only by comparing them with the syntax of the species."[36]

The writerly personality presents us with an especially fascinating case of an "idiom" unto itself. This idiom is constructed out of some dispositions that are innate to the species (the instinct for survival, for example), others that are inherited (a tendency toward humor, lyricism, or focus on facts), and still others that are what Allport calls "original dispositions." Among these original dispositions he singles out the capacity to learn.[37] These original dispositions are what most interest and, in fact, cheer me. In Woolf's case, the original disposition is an imaginative one, linking a capacity to learn to her ability to accommodate and give a voice to the many selves that coexist, sometimes on good, at other times on uneasy terms, within her. Woolf's original disposition to imagine states of being became so highly and subtly developed that she could even entertain the thought of selves she knew would never materialize, "the people one might have been; unborn selves," as Bernard calls them in *The Waves*.[38]

These unborn or nonselves also make up our sense of who we are by holding out possibilities of what we might yet become— the process is an open-ended rather than closed one. And this still does not take into account the phantasms of daydream and illness which entertain or affright the mind when the regulating and restraining powers of reason are relaxed or looking the other way or disabled altogether.

No one was more aware than Woolf, however, that the modern consciousness was more and more puzzled by the dilemma, and even the thought, of its own uniqueness. This puzzlement troubles Eleanor Pargiter in *The Years*, who, after a long life, is beginning to suspect that the self may have, in fact, no reliably discrete boundaries. Driving across London with her niece Peggy, she muses about the dilemma of her uniqueness, of *anyone's* uniqueness: "Where does she begin and where do I end, she thought. . . . They were two living people, driving across London; two sparks of life enclosed in two separate bodies; and those sparks of life enclosed in two separate bodies are at this moment, she thought, driving past a picture palace. But what is this moment; and what are we? The puzzle was too difficult for her to solve it."[39] Difficult for her to solve, but amazingly easy to pose, so commonplace has the question become of who and what we are in Woolf's fiction.

Bernard, one of the six speakers of her polyphonic novel, *The Waves*, seems to have been a character Woolf conceived primarily to engage with the dilemma of uniqueness and, by doing so, to explore—and suffer—the various original dispositions of Woolf's writerly personality. The main subject of Bernard's monologues is himself, a character who experiences and expresses the world as a novelist, not as a poet. These experiences are compared to a series of rooms in which a different aspect of his self is called upon to show and account for itself:

> There are many rooms—many Bernards. There was the charming, but weak; the strong, but supercilious; the brilliant, but remorseless; the very good fellow, but, I made no doubt, the awful bore; the sympathetic, but cold; the shabby, but—go into the next room—the foppish, worldly, and too well dressed. What I was to myself was different; was none of these. (W, 260)

What Bernard may be to himself exists apart from the Bernard who exists for and in the minds and hearts of other people. To his credit—or Woolf's—Bernard can contemplate the various, often egregiously contradictory appearances he assumes in the eyes of other people—weak, strong, brilliant, boring, sympathetic, cold, shabby, foppish—without jeopardizing his own relation to himself.

His conviction of the absolute difference between outer and inner self reiterates a common belief in Woolf's fiction first elaborated in *Mrs. Dalloway*, whose protagonist is struck and somewhat tormented by the difference between the private Clarissa and the public Mrs. Richard Dalloway. The splitting of the ego into public and private selves becomes the subject of playful asseveration in *Orlando*, whose beleaguered biographer-narrator, attempting to run down the inner character of his/her protean and apparently ageless protagonist, reports that the conscious self "has the power to desire, wishes to be nothing but one self. This is what some people call the true self, and it is, they say, compact of all the selves we have it in us to be; commanded and locked up the Captain self, the Key self, which amalgamates and controls them all" (O, 227). Here personality is figured not as a succession of interconnecting rooms, but as a command post that at once guards and superintends the various selves that we have it in us to be. Imagining the mind in this way is reassuring, but also disconcerting. It is one thing to propose that the true self is guarded by the Captain self, another to propose that the true self is locked up and commanded by the Key self. An imbalance of power, even a note of coercion, enters into this apparently light allegory of an Existential Fortress ruled by a Central Commander who keeps his charges in line. Who, after all, is this Key self who oversees our relations with others and regulates (whether with a firm or an indulgent hand, Woolf does not say) the interactions among all the selves that collectively make up our personality? Huxley's myth of the Whole Personality does not admit of any such executive being, which to my mind makes its more appealing, but at the same time less reassuring. Being—the true self—is managed and protected by sanctioned Authority—the Captain self. Although this true self may be "compact" of all the selves we have it in us to be, it is experienced not as a unity, but a constellation of selves, moods, dispositions, tempers.

In this respect, the writerly personality is subject to the same perceptual laws as the social personality described and analyzed by Proust:

> But even with respect to the most insignificant things in life, none of us constitutes a material whole, identical for everyone, which a person has only to go look up as though we were a book of specifications or a last testament; our social personality is a creation of the minds of others. Even the very simple act that we call "seeing a person we know" is in part an intellectual one. We fill the physical appearance of the individual we see with all the notions we have about him, and of the total picture that we form for ourselves, these notions certainly occupy the greater part. In the end they swell his cheeks so perfectly, follow the line of his nose in an adherence so exact, they do so well at nuancing the sonority of his voice as though the latter were only a transparent envelope that each time we see his face and hear this voice, it is these notions that we encounter again, that we hear.[40]

Reading someone we know—say, a writer as familiar to us as Woolf or Jane Austen or Keats—is in many ways no different from "seeing a person we know." In both cases what we think we know is an image of our own creation, a portrait in which all the various faces we have glimpsed, all the many intonations we have heard, are harmonized into a single impression. In this way, our relations to writers can be represented as Proust represents the social personality we create of our friends and acquaintances—as "a museum in which all the portraits from one period have a family look about them, a single tonality."[41]

In this museum in which are collected the various portraits we have gathered (and in truth fashioned) over our years of reading, we might see the various figments of the reader's—in this case my—imagination on display. The portraits of Woolf that I will display there have been assembled over thirty years of reading, teaching, writing, and thinking about a writer I know as well as I know anyone or anything. How well remains for the reader to decide. The essays that follow are offered as verbal portraits of Woolf's writerly personality; to my eyes, they share a similar tonality and have a family look about them. To put it another way, one more in line with the argument I have been unfolding, they all reflect a similar disposition. I have tried to harmonize these various dispositions, each of which I identify by assigning them the epithet that seems proper to them. These epithets are not meant to label Woolf's various selves, but to correspond to something essential, declarable, in her writerly personality. I derived these epithets from Woolf's own vocabulary for the self, stance, and public role that she assumed over the course of her writing life.

The Sibyl of the Drawing Room
Author
Critic
World Writer
Adventurer

What follows, then, is a series of epithetical, necessarily partial, but ultimately complementary portraits of Virginia Woolf's literary personality. Taken together, however, these part-portraits reveal Woolf's literary personality both in its public face—as author, critic, and world writer—and in its inner character—as a Sibyl and an adventurer. These writerly selves never work in complete isolation, of course. They collaborate and sometimes interfere with one another. They wander off on their own and then rejoin the chorus to which they contribute their own distinct voice.

It is impressive how well they worked together, given how different they could be. Assuming the mantle of critic or author or world writer, for example, Woolf spoke in a public voice; her private voice, like her innate disposition, was sibylline and adventurous. She thus sounds most like herself in those lyrical passages when she is musing or dreaming aloud, or in those humorous flights when she laughs at the dangers that intimidate others. I have come to believe that it was, finally, the adventurer in Woolf who took the role and assumed the responsibility of the Key self, the Captain self, that controlled and directed and inspired all the selves she had in her to be. It was the adventurer in her that made her restless, impelled her to ask, "Am I here, or am I there?" It was the adventurer in her who wondered whether "the true self" was "neither this nor that, neither here nor there, but something so varied and wandering that it is only when we give the rein to its wishes and let it take its way unimpeded that we are indeed ourselves?"[42] Another rhetorical question. For Woolf, in such adventurous moods, it is only for "convenience sake a man must be whole." The true self can only be experienced or captured or known when it is set free to imagine what it might be like to be, in no particular order, "a nomad wandering the desert, a mystic staring at the sky, a debauchee in the slums of San Francisco, a soldier heading a revolution, a pariah howling with skepticism and solitude."[43] Yet sometimes the most exciting adventures were those that were less sensational. So, for example, speaking in what we may provisionally take to be her "own" voice as an essayist, Woolf declared that "It is always an adventure to enter a new room; for the lives and characters of its owners have distilled their atmosphere into it; and directly we enter it we breast some new wave of emotion."[44]

I start, then, with Woolf's first adventure, her entrance into a new room and a new house that came to epitomize the ethos of modernist Bloomsbury, whose Sibyl she was eventually to become.

Woolf's Personalities

3

The Sibyl of the Drawing Room

WHERE THINGS START TO HAPPEN

"To begin with—admire our new address."[1] So wrote Virginia
Woolf on the eve of her move into a new house where she was
soon to discover—and enjoy—a different and decidedly new way
of life. There is still much to admire and indeed to celebrate in
Virginia Woolf's new address, 46 Gordon Square, and in the new
era it inaugurated in her personal and professional life as a writer.
Her arrival retrospectively came to mark the cultural ascendancy
of Bloomsbury not just as a London neighborhood, but as a mode
of living—irregular, informal, experimental—and a mode of
thinking and writing about the world—candid, irreverent, artful,
and sometimes pointedly arch—in a word, modern. Historically
Bloomsbury as a social grouping of artistic talents and attitudes
begins to form in that decisive year, 1904–1905, when Virginia
and Vanessa Stephen moved into 46 Gordon Square and Thoby
began his famous Thursday evenings, during which, amid now

legendary conversation, the Bloomsbury group began to congregate, coalesce, and consolidate itself.[2] Modernist Bloomsbury emerged with such astonishing rapidity that when Woolf came to write about these first exciting years a little less than two decades later, she already felt obliged to refer to that earlier time as "Old Bloomsbury."

But however admiringly, even reverentially, we might regard Woolf's relocation from the sedate Victorian confines of 22 Hyde Park Gate to the bustling modern precincts of 46 Gordon Square, we should not overlook her own initial misgivings about that momentous move. At first, the prospect of leaving 22 Hyde Park Gate for Bloomsbury did not appear cheering or even dimly inviting. "We have been tramping Bloomsbury this afternoon with Beatrice," she writes to Violet Dickinson in December 1903, "and staring up at dingy houses. There are lots to be had—but Lord how dreary! It seems so far away, and so cold and gloomy—but that was due to the dark and the cold I expect. Really we shall never get a house we like so well as this, but it is better to go."[3] These initial qualms were understandable, given the recent death of her father, Leslie Stephen, in the spring of 1904. Yet working as a counterirritant to the emotional inertia brought on by mourning was her growing impatience with the "queer mole like life" she was living at 22 Hyde Park Gate, within whose walls "the outside world seems to have ceased."[4] By the fall of 1904 she is eager for the move. Her distress swells to bitter complaint against the implacable Dr. Savage, the physician who treated her for the madness that overcame her that previous summer, for condemning her to convalescence in Cambridge before allowing her to settle into her new home. She writes to Violet Dickinson, who had nursed her that summer through her madness, protesting against the delay that will keep her from the free and full life awaiting her in 46 Gordon Square. She was eager to return to London, which to her represented the desired world of "my own home, and books, and pictures, and music."[5]

In her account of these days to the Memoir Club, Woolf would more calmly reflect on how Bloomsbury had retrospectively been endowed with the prestige of social and cultural myth. In her own recollections, she attempted to take a more reliable and human measure of Old Bloomsbury, one that would capture the relation between, and proportion of, inner circle and outer world. Old Bloomsbury, she proposed, was best understood and defined as a world within the world, as a "small concentrated world dwelling inside the much larger and looser world of dances and dinners."[6] The granite fact, to adopt Woolf's own idiom, that infuses and variegates the rainbow myth of Bloomsbury's "luster and illusion" (OB, 178) is that the "larger and looser" but also *earlier* world of dances and dinners that defined much of the life in Hyde Park Gate interpenetrated the life of Gordon Square, where it was brilliantly concentrated. For Woolf, it was out of those "concentrations"—in art, thought, and feeling—that modernist culture was made, or at least made possible. In such concentrations, Woolf found the dense social and psychological matter that she would eventually shape and reshape in the fiction to come: the nature and role of silence in human interchange; the changing relation of the sexes in modern times; the radical solitariness of the self; the comedy of social life. It was also within this world within a world that she found the materials and the inspiration to fashion her first literary avatar—the Sibyl of the drawing room.

So let us approach 46 Gordon Square as Woolf approached it both in life and in her recollections, through 22 Hyde Park Gate, honoring her insistence that "46 Gordon Square could never have meant what it did had not 22 Hyde Park Gate preceded it" (OB, 160). Her memoir of that name is primarily a recollection of her remorselessly conventional half-brother George Duckworth. He dominates her memoir as a dreaded creature, half god,[7] half faun, who looked at the world through the eyes of a pig.[8] His divinity was of the decidedly physical kind: "When Miss Willet of Brighton saw him 'throwing off his ulster' in the middle of her drawing room she was moved to write an Ode Comparing George Duckworth to the Hermes of Praxitiles" is the most hilarious instance of George's theophanic gestures that Woolf recalls. His religion, however, was social—he was a "saint" in sacrificing himself and his family to the "the ideals of a sportsman and an English gentleman."[9] The faun in George's nature, Woolf goes on to remark, "was at once sportive and demonstrative and thus often at variance with the self-sacrificing nature of the God": "It was quite a common thing to come into the drawing room and find George on his knees with his arms extended, addressing my mother, who might be adding up the weekly books, in tones of fervent adoration."[10] The social (disguised as moral) rectitude of the god and the emotional outbursts of the faun may have been at variance in nature, but they were united in George's singular determination to rise in the social scale. It was the physical god and social idolater who mercilessly dragged Woolf to teas, at homes, and dances, but it was the faun who, as reported in the scandalous penultimate paragraph of her memoir, visited her bedroom after a particularly ghastly evening spent dining with Lady Carnavaron and "took me in his arms." "Yes," she writes, "the old ladies of Kensington and

Belgravia never knew that George Duckworth was not only father and mother, brother and sister to those poor Stephen girls; he was their lover also."[11]

But George, who seemed to have usurped and monopolized all the family functions he was most unsuited and disqualified for, did not follow her to Gordon Square; he married. What Woolf did bring with her was training in the protocols of the drawing room and undiminished, if sometimes appalled, fascination with the people entertained and on display there. In her memoirs, George ironically emerges as a *genius loci* of the drawing room and its droll spectacles: he shines as Hermes, a god unveiled in the eyes of Miss Willet; he astonishes as the faun who "lavished caresses, endearments, enquiries and embraces as if, after forty years in the Australian bush, he had at last returned to the home of his youth and found an aged mother still alive to welcome him."[12] The drawing room is the entry into, but also the proscenium for, the dramatized past, since it was there that the traditions and manners of late Victorian family life were most extravagantly displayed.

This is made clear at the opening of "22 Hyde Park Gate," which begins with the disarming fiction that Woolf is resuming an interrupted conversation: "As I have said, the drawing room at Hyde Park Gate was divided by black folding doors picked out with thin lines of raspberry red. We were still much under the influence of Titian. Mounds of plush, Watts' portraits, busts shrined in crimson velvet, enriched the gloom of a room naturally dark and thickly shaded in summer by showers of Virginia Creeper."[13] Vanessa would introduce white and green chintzes and wash down the walls with plain distemper to brighten 46 Gordon Square, thus banishing the physical memory of velvet plush and somber Titian reds. In the first instance, then, Bloomsbury physically signified for Woolf a new brightness in surroundings and outlook that allowed her to see "things one had never seen in the darkness there—Watts pictures, Dutch cabinets, blue china," things that now "shone out for the first time in the drawing room at Gordon Square."[14] 22 Hyde Park Gate dimmed when it did not obscure the shiny aura of beautifully made objects.

But it was less the décor than the furnishing of the Hyde Park Gate drawing room that symbolized for her the kind of life that was lived and observed there. Woolf drew particular attention to the presence and importance of folding doors:

> How could family life have been carried on without them? As soon dispense with water-closets or bathrooms as with folding doors in a family of nine men and women, one of whom into the bargain was an idiot. Suddenly there would be a crisis—a servant dismissed, a lover rejected, pass books opened, or poor Mrs Tyndall who had lately poisoned her husband by mistake come for consolation.[15]

The folding doors were the essential stage machinery for mounting the theatricals of family life. On one side of the door, Woolf saw or imagined incidents—servants dismissed, lovers spurned, money lost or stolen, death by misadventure—lively and plentiful enough to provide narrative material for any number of sensationalist tales of domestic life.

But what engages her novelistic attention are the less "dark and agitated," more ordinary scenes of life that took place "on the other side of the door, especially on Sunday afternoon." There, Woolf recalls, life was cheerful enough. There round the oval tea table with its pink china shell full of spice buns would be found old General Beadle, talking of the Indian Mutiny; or Mr Haldane, or Sir Frederick Pollock—talking of all things under the sun; or old C. B. Clarke, whose name is given to three excessively rare Himalayan ferns, and Professor Wolstenholme, capable, if you interrupted him, of spouting two columns of tea not unmixed with sultanas through his nostrils; after which he would relapse into drowsy ursine torpor, the result of eating opium to which he been driven by the unkindness of his wife and the untimely death of his son Oliver who was eaten, somewhere off the coast of Coromandel, by a shark.[16]

Note the satiric transit of this remarkable sentence that takes us from spice buns feeding a crusty general, dreaming of empire, to a son who becomes the food for sharks. En route Woolf manages to evoke the imperial memories and convictions, the domestic tragedies, and the broad Dickensian comedy of Victorian patriarchs and pedants. Late Victorian and Edwardian society as it was encountered, accommodated, and entertained by a large, rambling, emotionally congested family converges in that drawing room.

How different the life encountered in the drawing room at Gordon Square, especially at Thoby's Thursday evenings, "the germ," Woolf would insist, "from which sprang all that since came to be called—in newspapers, in novels, in Germany, in France—even I daresay in Turkey and Timbuktu—by the name of Bloomsbury."[17] It was at these Thursday evenings that she heard talk of enormous interest and significance to her, talk about art that was at once abstract and technical, conversation shot through with wit and learning. In the company of ardent but unmannerly and often shabbily attired young men, Woolf gratefully remembers, "[a]ll that tremendous encumbrance of appearance and behavior which George had piled upon our first years vanished completely."[18] She particularly remarks the stark differences in life and feeling between the two drawing rooms: "In the world of the Booths and the Maxses we were not asked to use our brains much. Here we used nothing else. And part of the charm of those Thursday evenings was that they were astonishingly abstract."[19]

It was too abstract, in fact, to be altogether appealing to any but the most theoretical and rigorously logical mind, neither of which Woolf's mind could be said to be. In reporting her own reactions and contributions to those Bloomsbury evenings, Woolf appears less interested in recording people's actual words than in re-creating the rhythm of their exchanges, by which she seems to be taking the pulse, increasingly vigorous, of the new life germinating before her eyes:

> Now Hawtrey would say something; now Vanessa; now Saxon; now Clive; now Thoby. It filled me with wonder to watch those who were finally left in the argument piling stone upon stone, cautiously, accurately, long after it had completely soared above my sight. But if one could not say anything, one could listen. One had glimpses of something miraculous happening high up in the air.[20]

Woolf represents her young self at these occasions as a witness rather than cocreator of the conversational miracles she would later memorialize. This may be ascribed to the modesty inculcated

by the tea-table training of 22 Hyde Park Gate. Her disinclination
to scale the heights of argument may also represent the reluctance
of a young woman to speak before she has found her public voice.
One last explanation: Woolf may think it easier to evoke the excitement of those Thursday evenings from the point of view of
the young, unproven novelist (in this case, herself) beginning to
discover her human subject and her relation toward it. It is the
novelist, then, as much as the memoirist who chose not to repro-
duce the talk she heard, but to revisit instead her first vivid impressions of those who held forth on those Thursday evenings. And
what different as well as indelible impressions they were—the impressions made by the innocence and enthusiasm of Clive Bell,
by the wit of Lytton Strachey, who was, somewhat dauntingly,
"the essence of culture," a culture so condensed and rarefied that
he was capable of bursting into Thoby's room and crying, "Do
you hear the music of the spheres?" just before he fell into a dead
faint; and the singular impression made by an "astonishing fellow—a man who trembled perpetually all over . . . as eccentric,
as remarkable in his way as Bell and Strachey in theirs"[21]—a Jew
by the name of Leonard Woolf.

These droll recollections of the characters and talk that defined
Old Bloomsbury suggest that Thoby's Thursday evenings did not
so much disregard as transform the conventions of the Hyde Park
Gate drawing room. The talk Woolf was to hear would still be of
all things under the sun, but now it would be more "concentrated"; arguments would distill the essence of a question rather
than diffuse it in euphemism and evasion. Conversation was more
candid, but, as Woolf also recalls, it could languish in a way that
would be impossible at Hyde Park Gate. Thus 46 Gordon Square
succeeds but does not totally obliterate 22 Hyde Park Gate as a

scene of human interchange that interests her as much for its unspoken drama as for its open conversations. Woolf, whose literary personality and prospects are predominately identified with a room of her own, began her professional life as a writer equally absorbed with the life of the drawing room. Indeed it is arguable that without the training she received and the human dramas and behaviors she observed there, her fiction, however exalted in its visionary musings and lyrical transports, would have been humanly barren.

Modern Sibyls

That Woolf herself understood as much is evident in her first efforts at fiction, of which two short pieces are particularly valuable for the glimpse they give us of how she was imagining her former and present life from the new vantage point of 46 Gordon Square. The first was a short story entitled "Phyllis and Rosamond," written in 1906, a little over a year after Thoby's Thursday evenings had begun. The eponymous "heroines" are two sisters condemned, we are immediately informed, "to be what in the slang of the century is called the 'daughters at home.' "[22] In representing their social fate, Woolf seems to be imagining the life that would have been hers had she remained at 22 Hyde Park Gate. This being possibly so, it is telling that the most important thing Woolf has to say about them is that they

> seem indigenous to the drawing-room, as though, born in silk evening robes, they had never trod a rougher earth than the Turkey carpet, or reclined on harsher ground than the

arm chair or the sofa. To see them in a drawing-room full of well dressed men and women, is to see the merchant in the Stock Exchange, or the barrister in the Temple. This, every motion and word proclaims, is their native air; their place of business, their professional arena. Here, clearly, they practice the arts in which they have been instructed since childhood. Here, perhaps, they win their victories and earn their bread. (SF, 18)

Woolf is quick to denounce the condescension as well as incompleteness that mar this extended analogy, even if it is one of her own devising. The drawing room, however much it may seem their native habitat, is neither the exclusive nor the sole professional domain of daughters at home. The narrator contends that only by following these dutiful daughters through their daily rounds for many days would "you . . . be able to calculate the values of those impressions which are to be received by night in the drawing-room."

We are accustomed to associate Woolf's professional life as a writer with a room of one's own and five hundred pounds a year, her own calculation of how women might materially secure their intellectual and creative independence. But psychological liberation is not so easily achieved, a fact Woolf imaginatively acknowledged in conjuring the drawing room life of 22 Hyde Park Gate when she first tried her hand at fiction. It is in the Edwardian household, especially in the drawing room, that she could directly confront the problem of the novelist—how to calculate the value of those impressions that make up "the life of Monday and Tuesday," as she famously described the subject of her own work in "Modern Fiction."[23] 46 Gordon Square was inhabited and enlivened by two young women eager to institute all kinds of "reforms and experiments," from doing without table napkins and taking "coffee after dinner instead of tea at nine o'clock" to the bolder experiments of working as artists, writing and painting.[24] Yet when she came to write in her private room, Woolf chose not to represent the new world opening before her, but to return to the traditional life of women for whom the drawing room is a place of business and not speculative conversation.

In re-creating the world of the conventional drawing room, Woolf seems to be seeking a suitable place to practice her fledgling art of novelistic self-projection. Each sister gives voice to a different aspect of her own mind, character, and opinions. Rosamond is perhaps the closest to Woolf's writing self, endowed as she is with what we might call a proto-novelistic imagination. This is how the narrator describes her mental acuity: "Rosamond, possessed of shrewd and capable brains, had been driven to feed them exclusively upon the human character and as her science was but little obscured by personal prejudice, her results were generally trustworthy" (SF, 22). Rosamond certainly lacks a room of her own, and perhaps (we will never know) the art to express her impressions in writing. Woolf nevertheless praises her "science" of character-reading for its impartiality and accuracy.

If Rosamond's science is a projection and prototype of Woolf's own novelistic art of reading and judging character, Phyllis's emotionalism anticipates the indignation that will animate Woolf's satires against the regime of the traditional drawing room, where women possessed of shrewd and capable brains are routinely discouraged or suppressed. She dramatizes and exploits Phyllis's equally shrewd if more partial judgment of character in the concluding episode, a visit the sisters pay to the Tristrams. The Tristrams are a family that regards love not as "something induced by certain calculated actions" but as "a robust, ingenuous thing which stood out in the daylight, naked and solid, to be tapped and scrutinised as you thought best" (SF, 25–26). The family name is worth pausing over. Like Joyce's choice of Dedalus as the name of his young fictional alter-ego, Tristram seems at once symbol and prophecy of Woolf's nascent artistic identity. It conjures up the ghost of Sterne, the creator of *Tristram Shandy*, and the Wagner of *Tristan and Isolde*, representatives, respectively, of the humorist and the high romantic fabulist that coexisted within her own imagination. The Tristrams, like the Stephen sisters after 1904, live in "a distant and unfashionable quarter of London" (SF, 24) known as Bloomsbury. To describe how Bloomsbury might appear to sheltered maidens from Kensington (of whom, of course, Woolf once counted herself), Woolf turns to the more fanciful Phyllis, who, with less novelistic science than her sister, is both envious of and exhilarated by the prospect of a different pattern and tempo of life beyond the pillars of Belgravia and South Kensington:

> That was one of the many enviable parts of their lot. The stucco fronts, the irreproachable rows of Belgravia and South Kensington seemed to Phyllis the type of her lot; of a life trained to grow in an ugly pattern to match the staid ugliness of its fellows. But if one lived here in Bloomsbury, she began to theorise waving with her hand as her cab passed through the great tranquil squares, beneath the pale green of umbrageous trees, one might grow up as one liked. There was room, and freedom, and in the roar and splendour of the Strand she read the live realities of the world from which her stucco and her pillars protected her so completely. (SF, 24)

Phyllis, whose name literally means green leaf, is a poignant shadow figure of Woolf's own exultant entry into modernist territory. Her hungry and clamoring spirit welcomes the new sense of human possibility revealed to her. The sensationalist dramas of abandoned lovers and disgraced servants enacted in the staid drawings rooms of Kensington instantly become dated when exposed to the robust roar and vital splendor of the Strand.

It is from Phyllis's awed and increasingly intimidated perspective that Woolf attempts her first fictional account of the conversations that came to define and distinguish the cultural life of Old Bloomsbury:

> The talk was of certain pictures then being shown, and their merits were discussed from a somewhat technical standpoint. Where was Phyllis to begin? She had seen them; but she knew that her platitudes would never stand the test of question and criticism to which they would be exposed. Nor, she knew, was there any scope here for those feminine graces which could veil so much. The time was passed; for the discussion was hot and serious, and no one of the combatants wished to be tripped by illogical devices. So she sat and watched, feeling like a bird with wings pinioned; and more acutely, because more genuinely, uncomfortable than she had ever been at ball or play. She repeated to herself the little bitter axiom that she had fallen between two stools; and tried meanwhile to use her brains soberly upon what was being said. (SF, 24–25)

Although Woolf's personal circumstances and modern outlook align her with "this strange new point of view" of the Tristrams, she is more concerned, even anxious, to describe how the uncensored conversations and frank opinions entertained in a Bloomsbury drawing room appear to those outside, if drawn to, such enlightened and ebullient society. The narrator thus reports how Rosamond and Phyllis, amazed by the new ideas and attitudes they encounter, quietly listen "unconscious of their own silence, like people shut out from some merrymaking in the cold and wind; invisible to the feasters within" (SF, 26).

I find it symptomatic that one of Woolf's first completed sketches after settling into Bloomsbury involves a story of two young women who long for a modernity they feel entirely unprepared for, who fall between two stools. I am not suggesting that Woolf was personally unsettled or unnerved within the small, concentrated society that opened up for her in Gordon Square. On the contrary, I am marveling that she felt secure enough to explore imaginatively what was both inside and outside the new world of Old Bloomsbury. In "Phyllis and Rosamond," Woolf is actively experimenting with the personally discomfiting but narratively rewarding effects of bilocation. Bilocation is the positive counterpart to falling between two stools. Falling between two stools lands one in an indefinite and often inglorious mental or social space between two established and equally attractive or dismaying positions. Those adept in bilocation occupy both, rather than fall between, those positions. By exercising her skill in bilocation, Woolf narratively situates herself both within and outside of the human scene she is representing. In the Tristrams' drawing room, she transparently represents her newfound life in Bloomsbury; in Sylvia Tristram, the youngest daughter, she depicts the modern (sympathetic) female artist she aspired to be—substantial in character, abstract in thought, in Phyllis's words, "a solid woman in spite of her impersonal generalisations" (SF, 26). Sylvia, however, has as much to learn from Phyllis and Rosamond as they from her. She suddenly realizes that she "had never considered the Hibberts as human beings before; but had called them 'young ladies,' " a "mistake" she admits that she is eager to revise "both from vanity and from real curiosity." Neither her vanity nor her curiosity leads her to the reality of the Hibberts' lives, as Woolf makes clear to us when Sylvia somewhat presumptuously suggests to Rosamond and Phyllis that "we are sisters": "O no, we're not sisters," Phyllis bitterly objects; "at least I pity you if we are. You see, we are brought up just to come out in the evening and make pretty speeches and, well, marry I suppose, and of course we might have gone to college if we'd wanted to; but as we didn't we're just accomplished" (SF, 27). As this exchange poignantly shows, it is Phyllis, not Sylvia, who is the realist, in both the common and the novelistic sense of the word, in identifying who she really is.

This sketch is followed in 1909 by "Memoirs of a Novelist," in which Bloomsbury reappears in a somewhat different light. "Memoirs of a Novelist" is a fictional review of a biography of an imaginary female novelist named Miss Willatt. Woolf's tone in this fanciful portrait is low and broad enough for satire, but close enough to its (imaginary) human subject to capture the pathos of Miss Willatt's fretful and somewhat misbegotten creative endeavors. The following passage makes this comically clear:

It does not seem, to judge by appearances, that the world has so far made use of its right to know about Miss Willatt. The volumes had got themselves wedged between Sturm "On the Beauties of Nature" and the "Veterinary Surgeon's

Manual" on the outside shelf, where the gas cracks and the dust grimes them, and people may read so long as the boy lets them. Almost unconsciously one begins to confuse Miss Willatt with her remains and to condescend a little to these shabby, slipshod volumes.[25]

The narrator-reviewer acknowledges, but ultimately resists, the urge to condescend to those prevented by death from becoming as enlightened as we, the living, so self-assuredly are. She is equally impatient, however, with the biographer's idyllic account of Miss Willatt's youth. She offers her own suppositions of what Miss Willat's youthful character might have been, suppositions that soon take the form of self-projection. Item in point: taking up the characterization of Miss Willatt as a "shy awkward girl much given to mooning," the reviewer-narrator goes on to imagine her as a young woman who

walked in to pigsties, and read history instead of fiction, did not enjoy her first ball. . . . She found some angle in the great ball room where she could half hide her large figure, and there she sat waiting to be asked to dance. She fixed her eyes upon the festoons which draped the city arms and tried to fancy that she sat on a rock with bees humming round her; she bethought her how no one in that room perhaps knew as well as she did what was meant by the Oath of Uniformity; then she thought how in sixty years, or less perhaps, the worm would feed upon them all; then she wondered whether somehow before that day, every man now dancing there would not have reason to respect her. (SF, 72)

The rough biographical similarities between the imaginary Miss Willatt and her creator Miss Stephen—both shy, mooning young women embarrassed by their body, dreaming of becoming historians, beginning their creative life in earnest after the death of a father—are interesting only to the extent that they reveal how even at this early stage in her career Woolf possessed not just the talent, but the courage, for self-parody.

Woolf is especially impressive when she confronts—and proceeds to mock—her own proclivities toward mystical flights of imagination. She is, in fact, quite remorseless in describing how Miss Willatt, who in her youth could clarify and correct any misapprehensions about the Uniformity Law, matures into an enormously stout seer who, "in her hot little drawing-room with the spotted wall paper," presides over "intimate conversations about 'the Soul' ": " 'The Soul' became her province, and she deserted the Southern plains for a strange country draped in eternal twilight, where there are qualities without bodies" (SF, 77). In Miss Willatt, Woolf entertains the possibility of a new writerly incarnation—the Sibyl of the drawing room: " 'We felt often that we had a Sibyl among us,' " one of Miss Willatt's acolytes testifies, a remark that inspires the narrator to speculate that "if Sibyls are only half inspired, conscious of the folly of their disciples, sorry for them, very vain of their applause and much muddled in their own brains all at once, then Miss Willatt was a Sibyl too" (SF, 78). Miss Willatt's elevation to Sibyl-hood is at once comic and doleful: comic in her vainglorious soulfulness, doleful in "the unhappy view that it gives of the spiritual state of Bloomsbury at this period—when Miss Willatt brooded in Woburn Square like some gorged spider at the centre of her web, and all along the filaments unhappy women came running, slight hen-like figures, frightened by the sun and the carts and the dreadful world, and longing to hide themselves from the entire panorama in the shade of Miss Willatt's skirts" (SF, 78).

Today we associate Bloomsbury with a happier, certainly less gloomy spiritual state, one in which women are no longer frightened by the sun or spooked by the bogeys and commotions of the "dreadful world." Imaginative courage to face and represent the world, dreadful or not, is not a moral gift bestowed by the accidents of birth and temperament, however. It is achieved as much as inherited. For Woolf, imaginative courage is often found through the sound and sense of laughter. Woolf knew the value of laughter early on and commented on it persuasively in an essay that also belongs to the story of Woolf's move to Bloomsbury. In "The Value of Laughter," she proposed that "there are some things that are beyond words and not beneath them and laughter is one of these."[26] Woolf then went on to elaborate a distinction that I believe is key to understanding Bloomsburyean Woolf and all the writing to come after:

> Humour is of the heights; the rarest minds alone can climb the pinnacle whence the whole of life can be viewed as in a panorama; but comedy walks the highways and reflects the trivial and accidental—the venial faults and peculiarities of all who pass in its bright little mirror. Laughter more than anything else preserves our sense of proportion; it is for ever reminding us that we are but human, that no man is quite a hero or entirely a villain.[27]

Bloomsbury released and confirmed the power of laughter in Woolf's spiritual outlook. It helped her maintain a sense of proportion, grounded her,[28] reminded her of what it is to be all too human. But it did something else as well. It reinforced her sense of herself as a female novelist writing in the tradition of women who had profited from their long and demanding training in the science of character-reading. "I believe," Woolf affirmed, "that the verdict that women pass upon character will not be revoked at the Day of Judgment."[29] For Woolf, training in these novelistic arts of judgment had come, as it had for Rosamond, as it had for so many of her literary mothers, in the drawing room.

Woolf would resort without hesitation to the female traditions preserved and untiringly practiced in the drawing room throughout her career to enhance her illusionist art and to sharpen her powers of observation and judgment. She does so most conventionally in *Night and Day*, a novel dedicated to her sister Vanessa (whose heroine, Katherine Hilbery, is modeled upon her) that begins in the drawing room and in some senses never fully leaves it. Its presiding Sibyl is Mrs. Hilbery, the daughter of an eminent Victorian man of letters whose face, "shrunken and aquiline," is softened by "the large blue eyes, at once sagacious and innocent, which seemed to regard the world with the enormous desire that it should behave itself nobly, and the entire confidence that it could so, if it would only take the pains."[30]

Neither sagacity nor innocence is suggested by Woolf's most searching and sardonic novelistic portrait of the "perfect hostess," as Peter Walsh sneeringly calls the worldly Clarissa Dalloway. Clarissa is at first dismayed by the epithet, but ultimately embraces it as a creditable, even noble office:

Oh, it was very queer. Here was So-and-so in South Kensington; some one up in Bayswater; and some else, say, in Mayfair. And she felt quite continuously a sense of their existence; and she felt what a waste; and she felt what a pity; and she felt if only they could be bought together; so she did it. And it was an offering; to combine, to create; but to whom?

An offering for the sake of offering, perhaps. Anyhow, it was her gift.[31]

The drawing room becomes a kind of ritual space where the society hostess makes her ceremonial offerings to the gods of amity, where she propitiates those whom life has kept separate, isolated, alone.

Woolf became so confident in the novelistic uses of the drawing room as a ritualistic space that she could afford to mock her own sibylline powers in *Orlando*:

The hostess is our modern Sibyl. She is a witch who lays her guests under a spell. In this house they think themselves happy; in that witty; in a third profound. It is all an illusion (which is nothing against it, for illusions are the most valuable and necessary of all things, and she who can create one is among the world's greatest benefactors), but as it is notorious that illusions are shattered by conflict with reality, so no real happiness, no real wit, no real profundity are tolerated where the illusion prevails. (O, 146)

The drawing room has become a magical theater, in which Woolf, humorously wielding the power of the modern Sibyl, creates the illusion, at once as necessary and ultimately as insubstantial as any of Prospero's magical shows, that happiness, wit, and even profundity are within our powers if only we would, as Mrs. Hilbery believes, take the pains. The conversational miracles Woolf observed at Thoby's Thursday evenings may have inspired such beliefs. Still, they were beliefs, not realities. As Sibyl of the drawing room, Woolf lives out a novelistic fantasy of being among the world's greatest benefactors. In exchange for our indulgence as readers, she offers us the much greater gift of exposing the emptiness of that fantasy, of any fantasy, that promises us untroubled happiness, unfailing wit, and fathomless profundity. Her years in the drawing room and her integrity as a writer had taught her the vanity of any such hopes.

Nevertheless, Woolf would return for one final time to the drawing room as a site of remarkable transformation scenes in the tableau that closes her last novel, *Between the Acts*. In the novel's concluding page, the family of Pointz Hall foregathers before retiring for the long dark night ahead. The year is 1939, the place is outside London. Although there have been several complaints by various characters in the novel that surely it is time that someone invented a new plot or that the author come out of the bushes, the old plots, we come to understand, will have to suffice, and the author will not be showing herself, nor courting applause, much less celebrity, any time soon. Only at the moment when Isa, the novel's abortive poet and restless seeker after latent and larger meanings, lets her sewing drop does a new human vista emerge:

> The great hooded chairs had become enormous. And Giles too. And Isa too against the window. The window was all sky without colour. The house had lost its shelter. It was night before roads were made, or houses. It was the night that dwellers in caves had watched from some high place among the rocks. Then the curtain rose. They spoke. (BA, 219)

We do not of course hear these first words. But I like to think that those spoken words might include snatches of conversation that Woolf overheard at Thoby's Thursday evenings, words, at any rate, punctuated by bursts of laughter. Even without knowing what those words might be, we might respond to their power. Through them, Woolf speaks to us in her last work as a sublime humorist who "alone can climb the pinnacle whence the whole of life can be viewed as in a panorama." From that pinnacle she beheld the entire human panorama from the temporary shelter of the present moment back to the night before roads were made.

But for Woolf the climb to that pinnacle begins in the drawing room. If Sibyls are half visionaries in whose gaze the whole of life is comprehended and half comic seers conscious of "all the hideous excrescences that have overgrown our modern life, its pomps and conventions and dreary solemnities,"[32] then Virginia Woolf is a Sibyl, too. In her last fiction, indeed, she appears as the most humorous incarnation of that Bloomsburyean figure: the Sibyl of the drawing room.

4

The Author

Words

In 1915, under the terms of the National Registration Act, Virginia Woolf was registered by her husband Leonard as an "author." [1] This official classification seems straightforward enough. The literary vocation of Virginia Woolf seems a public fact, now as then, to which we might hardly give a second thought, especially given the avalanche of work on her literary ideas, politics, psychology, autobiographical and critical writings that began with Quentin Bell's 1975 biography of his aunt and gathered force and momentum with the subsequent publication of her complete diaries, letters, and collected essays. In truth, everything about Virginia Woolf, author, is in danger of becoming benignly familiar to common readers as well as professional critics—her life, her critical precepts, her feminist politics, the distinctive rhythms of her prose.

Yet just when we believe Woolf is securely enshrined in the niche (modern, author, female) assigned her, we encounter, as we do in a radio address entitled "Craftsmanship," a writer whose relationship to words strikes us as either so advanced or so primitive as to confound any settled view we might have of her. Woolf begins this talk, part of a series devoted to the theme "Why Words Fail Us," by confessing to a limited knowledge of her subject: "Now we know little that is certain about words," she disingenuously remarks, "but this we do know—words never make anything that is useful; and words are the only things that tell the truth and nothing but the truth."[2] This is an extraordinary, even preposterous claim, and we hardly know how to respond to it. First, there is the questionable assertion, which Woolf treats as incontrovertible fact, that words never make anything useful. But of course they do—they are used to make contracts and treaties, manuals and guides, to name only a few of the useful forms words may take, as Woolf elsewhere openly acknowledges.[3] We can only surmise that she is deliberately exaggerating both the total uselessness and the absolute truth-value of words in order to dramatize a rather more reasonable and subtle point—namely, that words don't fail us; we fail them. Perhaps such a judgment also underlies her claim that words always tell the truth and nothing but the truth. She speaks in legal terms, as if words themselves were perpetually "under oath," while it is we, she insinuates, who lie and deceive and employ words for fraudulent ends.

Not everyone believes words have no useful function to perform. Few, truth be told, use them with such strict regard for truth. Only authors do. No one exemplifies this dictum better than Woolf herself. In assessing what was singular and impracticable, even iconoclastic, about her relationship to words, it is worth recalling, first of all, the etymological origin of authorship in "augere," to increase. An author is a creator, then, in the sense that writing *adds* something to our store of information about the world, enlarges the range of experience allotted us, and expands our sense of what words can mean and what they can do when liberated from the utilitarian purposes to which we commonly enlist them.

Certainly no one could accuse Woolf of making words perform any practical work.[4] The language of authorship for her is a distinctly literary language that pays little attention to the practical usages to which words might be put in ordinary life. It is in fact surprising how little of her feeling for words is aroused by the colloquialisms and neologisms peculiar to modern times. Her fictional language remains relatively unaffected by the slang heard in the streets, the fashionable argot of the upper classes, or the specialized jargon of scientific or economic elites. Although she does not flinch before lewd realities, obscene words are not part of her vocabulary, as they are, for example, for that garrulous marvel of modern fiction, Molly Bloom. Nor does Woolf adapt the terminology being spawned by modern physics, as Lawrence did the language of electromagnetism in *Women in Love,* to express her vision of reality.

Perhaps most surprising, given her repeated declarations that modern fiction is rightly concerned with illuminating the "dark places of psychology," is the relatively traditional language Woolf uses in her own representations of the mind, what it contains, and what it produces. Woolf speaks of the mind's sensations and impressions in a way that makes her more conversant with Hume and Locke than with modern psychologists and their talk of libido and drives. Even Woolf's use of the word "atoms" in her famous description of how little pellets of perception fall upon the mind like an "incessant shower"[5] is one that Democritus, the fifth-century philosopher who gave the word its modern meaning, might have understood. While she was certainly aware of psychoanalysis and reviewed the newest instances of Freudian fiction (the title of one of her reviews),[6] she avoided radically assimilating its language to her own. Her characters may exhibit the *symptoms* of the mental afflictions that preoccupy modern psychology, but neither they nor Woolf's narrators make explicit reference to the diagnostic *nomenclature* of psychoanalysis. Words like hysteria, complex, repression, trauma, melancholia, fetishism, and cathexis are either absent or rarely encountered in her fiction, and even then, as Hermione Lee observes, only in the late work of the 1930s. Perhaps Woolf found these words too clinically "useful"; perhaps she was not convinced of their truth-value. Whatever her reasons, Woolf, who, as Lee also remarks, was caught between "competing narratives of mental illness—Darwinian, moralistic, Freudian," preferred to create "an original language of her own . . . which could explain her illness to her and give it value."[7]

Virginia Woolf, author, might thus justly be characterized as a radical conservative in practicing her craft. The most obvious sign of her linguistic conservatism is that, unlike Joyce, she never played too freely with the material form of words. Perhaps she feared that their truth-content might leak out if words were broken up into their component parts or if their letters were rearranged to form anagrams or neologisms in the jocular style of the more free-wheeling modernists. Certainly she never contemplated *inventing* a language, as Joyce did in *Finnegans Wake,* that would amalgamate all known forms of expression from the litter/

letter of post-Babelian humanity. Nor on a more modest scale
does she indulge in wordplay of the kind that entrances and
amuses. The pun hardly appears in her fiction, whereas for a writer
like Beckett, who once affirmed "In the beginning was the pun,"[8]
there could be no authorship without this initial doubleness and
potential duplicity at the very heart of language.

Only rarely—as in the skywriting sequence of *Mrs. Dalloway*—
did Woolf stage the kind of wordplay in which *Ulysses* displays its
irreverent modernism:

> Dropping dead down the aeroplane soared straight up,
> curved in a loop, raced, sank, rose and whatever it did, wher-
> ever it went, out fluttered behind it a thick ruffled bar of
> white smoke which curled and writhed upon the sky in let-
> ters. But what letters? A C was it? An E, then an L? Only
> for a moment did they lie still; they moved and melted and
> were rubbed out up in the sky and the aeroplane shot further
> away and again, in a fresh space of sky began writing a K,
> an E, a Y perhaps. (MD, 29)

The "K E (Y?)" to this enigmatic script, as it transpires, proves to
be nothing more lofty than an advertisement. Woolf doubtless
intended a sly jab at the dream entertained by Joyce's imaginative
hero, the adman Leopold Bloom, whose habitual "final meditations" before retiring to bed center on "some one sole unique
advertisement to cause passers to stop in wonder, a poster novelty,
with all extraneous accretions excluded, reduced to its simplest
and most efficient terms not exceeding the span of casual vision
and congruent with the velocity of modern life."[9] The novelty of

skywriting,[10] aside from its unusual choice of writing implement, is that words are no sooner formed than they dissolve. Though it might satisfy Bloom's criteria of being consonant with the velocity of modern life, the simple, efficient, and wondrous message written on air proves not only an instantaneous, but a radically unstable one. While ground-gazers stutter out the letters, the plane, using the sky as parchment, is transformed into a vehicle for ethereal authorship, "the symbol of something which has soared beyond seeking and questing and knocking of words together and has become all spirit, disembodied, ghostly" (MD, 42).

Woolf would later return to more homely ground to dramatize how language might be used *before* the seeking and questing and knocking of words together. Here, for example, is a mundane scene from *Between the Acts,* a novel urgently concerned with recovering a primordial relation to words:

> The nurses after breakfast were trundling the perambulator up and down the terrace; and as they trundled they were talking—not shaping pellets of information or handing ideas from one to another, but rolling words, like sweets on their tongues; which, as they thinned to transparency, gave off pink, green and sweetness. (BA, 10)

The custodians of the young are also conservators and curators of what we might classify as a form of Ur-language, language before it becomes devoted to practical ends, like recording information or transmitting ideas. The nurses are not "coining" words into expressive shapes, as Woolf speculates the people of Babel did in the beginning, "taking . . . pain in one hand, and a lump of pure sound in the other."[11] On the contrary, their talk conveys nothing of substance. Their words are verbal confections that, as they liquefy, release their sweetness and color. No meaning is "released" by the increasingly transparent nuggets of sound that roll off the nurses's tongues, yet their words contain a reality as palpable, as nutritive for the mind, hungry for sensations, as any words graven in tablets of indigestible stone.

These last examples suggest that Virginia Woolf's relationship with words was never secure, nor was it even healthy, if health is measured by a pragmatic determination to let words retain the meanings and practical uses they have in common parlance. But there are other ways of assessing the health of an organism or of a literary style. Vitality, for one; energy for adventure, for another. The writer's metabolism is delicate, however, no matter how robust her imaginings. She must be willing to relinquish those words or verbal manners, no matter how reassuring and cherished, that have become burdensome or inexpressive of what the heart really feels or the mind actually sees. We cannot understand, much less appreciate, how much Woolf extended the boundaries of modern writing unless we remark how much she was willing to forgo, as well as preserve, in making her unique representations of the world.

An irony confronts us, then, at the outset of any consideration of the literary language fashioned by Virginia Woolf, the author of novels, essays, political tracts, one biography (two, if you count *Flush*, and why shouldn't we?), and many abbreviated literary portraits, including the partial self-portraits collected in *Moments of Being*. The irony, which has the potential of ripening into a paradox, is this: Virginia Woolf is a writer who increased our sense of what writing is by taking away as much as she bestowed.

VOICES

Nowhere does this irony resonate more plangently than in the pages of Erich Auerbach's magisterial history of realism in Western literature, *Mimesis*. When Auerbach, marooned in Turkey during the Second World War, sought a work representative of the modernist epoch, he chose *To the Lighthouse*. At the time it must have seemed an odd, even eccentric, choice. Indeed, his initial effort to describe what arrests his attention as "new" in Woolf's prose style suggests that he selected Woolf's novel for what was in fact anomalous in her rendering of reality. In the course of summarizing the events and motifs represented in a passage he has extracted for analysis, he suddenly comes upon a phrase, unremarkable in itself, that confounds him. It is a phrase describing Mrs. Ramsay in a certain mood and in a certain light: "Never did anybody look so sad." Auerbach, as if taken aback, almost blurts out the question that opens the following paragraph: "Who is speaking in this paragraph?" His question is not a rhetorical one, although it may appear at first to be one. He poses this question as if in finding an answer he might unlock the mystery of narrative speech itself, by which not only human beings, but entire societies and even worlds are predicated and brought to life.

Auerbach is beginning to feel, somewhat urgently, the absence of a familiar, reassuring presence who has accompanied him as he read through Western literature from its founding texts, the Bible and Homer's *Odyssey*, to the modern realist works of Cervantes, Stendhal, and Flaubert—the figure of the author. He tentatively concludes that while it is Virginia Woolf, the author, speaking, "she does not seem to bear in mind that she is the author and hence

ought to know how matters stand with her characters." Struck by
the uncertainty with which the author conveys the impressions
and feelings that fill the consciousness of her characters, Auerbach
openly wonders at the "doubtful, obscure suppositions" that re-
place the objective certainties of the traditional narrator who presents and interprets his characters with unshaken confidence. Could
these suppositious musings about a woman looking so sad origi-
nate in a nonhuman order? He ventures that these speakers are not

> human beings at all but spirits between heaven and earth,
> nameless spirits capable of penetrating the depths of the
> human soul, capable too of knowing something about it,
> but not of attaining clarity as to what is in process there,
> with the result that what they report has a doubtful ring,
> comparable in a way to those "certain airs, detached from
> the body of the wind," which in a later passage move about
> the house at night, "questioning and wondering."[12]

In passages such as this one that perplex Auerbach, Woolf extended modern authorship to the verge where the distinct "voice
of the author"—let us call it the voice of the narrative person,
whether young or old, male or female, well- or ill-educated—
merges with and is absorbed into a language "voiced" by no one
we can easily identify, much less locate. Late in her life, Woolf
thought that authors might be divided into two kinds: the ventriloquists and soliloquists.[13] Woolf's own progress as an author
might be charted as a series of attempts to orchestrate the two
kinds of literary performance not harmonically, but in counter-
point. Her fictions are structured by alternating currents of poetic
soliloquy and novelistic impersonation. The strange consonance
Woolf makes of their fundamental differences helps explain the

peculiar affect of Woolf's narrative voice, at once so intimate and confiding, yet capable of cool, even savagely ironic, detachment.[14]

Let us first parse the ventriloquist's mode of authorship, one rooted in the common language of the people. It is as a ventriloquist that Woolf is most conscious of her ties to tradition. It is as a ventriloquist, we might say, that she offered her famous maxim on the language of masterpieces in *A Room of One's Own:* "For masterpieces are not single and solitary births; they are the outcome of many years of thinking in common, of thinking by the body of the people, so that the experience of the mass is behind the single voice."[15] Woolf had a distinct model for the single voice expressing the experience of the many: the chorus in Greek tragedy, steeped in convention, suspicious of moral renegades and wary of any radical departure from the established order of things. The voice of the chorus is thus not to be confused with the voice of mass or popular culture. It is not the voice of the crowd or of the faceless masses. Her fiction shares little of the literary naturalist's "lowbrow" fascination with the pungent, often racy language and entertainments of modern popular culture. What unites the chorus and shapes their common language are the shared values that emerge out of a long and common experience of living and thinking together, not the tastes bred by the fashions of the lively, but fugitive moment. This choric voice begins sounding in *Mrs. Dalloway,* dissolves in the lyric meditations of *The Waves,* is revived in *The Years,* only to be fragmented and dispersed into the "stray voices, voices without bodies, symbolical voices" (BA, 151) that sound, alternately stentorian and muffled, throughout *Between the Acts.* This last was the novel in which Woolf set out to test the limits of her negative capability, not so much by suspending as by rejecting entirely "the damned egotistical self"[16] she discerned and disliked in the writing of Joyce and Dorothy

Richardson, two pioneers of the "stream-of-consciousness" technique that tracked the mind's undifferentiated flow of thoughts and sensations.

Woolf, for her part, was busy devising a form supple enough to allow her to write indiscriminately about "anything that comes into my head," while avoiding the shoals of egotism on which, to her mind, so much modern writing foundered. Her diary records her determination to discuss

> all literature in connection with real little incongruous living humour: & anything that comes into my head; but "I" rejected: "We" substituted: to whom at the end there shall be an invocation? "We" . . . composed of many different things . . . we all life, all art, all waifs and strays—a rambling capricious but somehow unified whole—the present state of my mind?[17]

The novelist's rambling, capricious mind, so attuned to the "many different things" that combine to form the plural "We," seems especially susceptible to the currents of collective emotion. Woolf's prose is frequently infected by the contagion of group feeling, which alters the rhythm and frequently accelerates the momentum of her sentences.

We can see such contagion at work in Woolf's description of the royal cavalcade in *Mrs. Dalloway.* As it makes its way through London, the car "confers emotion, vainly, on commoners out for a drive." The word "vainly," placed at a strategic juncture in the sentence, make us pause before committing ourselves to the emotion slowly gathering momentum in the streets. By introducing this slight "hitch" in the onward motion of the caravan (and, of course, of the sentence that describes its passing), she alerts us to the limits, as well as to the waywardness, of the emotion aroused by the regalia of royalty (which itself may be judged a vanity in the Biblical sense). The emotion, when it is finally allowed its unconstrained expression, takes the infectious form of rumor. The narrator accordingly begins to trace, quickly and nimbly, the associative chain that links all those commoners who

> let rumour accumulate in their veins and thrill the nerves in their thighs at the thought of Royalty looking at them; the Queen bowing; the Prince saluting; at the thought of the heavenly life divinely bestowed upon Kings; of the equerries and deep curtsies; of the Queen's old doll's house; of Princess Mary married to an Englishman, and the Prince—ah! the Prince! who took wonderfully, they said, after Old King Edward, but was ever so much slimmer. (MD, 20–21)

The thoughts and words represented here are not those of a homogenized crowd, but of a highly differentiated yet amiably communicative "we." Individual responses, while still audible, are subsumed into a continuous train of thought that moves in comic synchrony with the motor car. The narrator exults in this demonstration that thought, especially as it transmits itself from mind to excited mind, can move so quickly—and so far! From the streets it ventures into the private chambers where the Queen keeps her old doll's house; once there it ranges freely and not all that illogically from the venerable conception of society and state embodied in the divine existence of kings to the more mundane fascination with generational fluctuations in the royal avoirdupois.

This exuberant rush of communal fantasy is given an extra lift by that gratified exclamation—ah!—that temporarily arrests the flow of associations, an effect so captivating yet so unexpected that we might be forgiven for wondering if it is not excitement itself crying out in the thrill of the moment. Or perhaps we are hearing the voice of rumor that has accumulated long enough in the veins of the onlookers and now must release that little yelp of surprised and satisfied delight. Joyce makes such exclamatory sounds parts of the *dramatis personae* in the hallucinatory drama staged in "Circe," the Nighttown episode of *Ulysses*. "The Hue and Cry" along with "The Call" and "The Answer" are personified and given speaking parts, as are "The Echo" and "Chimes." But Woolf's tactic is at once more subtle and more strange. The "ah" uttered here is not meant to signal, as Joyce's auditory hallucinations do, a schizophrenic breakdown in narration. Woolf is out to capture something at large in the human world but audible only to the novelistic inner ear, like "the unheard rhythm of their own wild hearts" (BA, 65) to which only the narrator of *Between the Acts* is attuned.

At other times the ventriloquizer's language seems to issue not from the body of the people but, as Auerbach first surmised, from the nonhuman world that predated and will outlast us. In such moments, "I" is rejected in order that, literally it would seem, the divinities who shape our ends can be heard. Here, for example, is what the god of rain, if it exists, might say, as translated by the narrator of *The Years*:

> . . . the god of rain, if there were a god, was thinking Let it not be restricted to the very wise, the very great, but let all breathing kind, the munchers and the chewers, the ignorant,

the unhappy, those who toil in the furnace making innumer-
able copies of the same pot, those who bore red hot minds
through contorted letters and also Mrs. Jones in the alley,
share my bounty. (Y, 48)

Joining the modern, itemizing language of the catalog with the
traditional strains of litany, the rain god extends his blessing on
"all breathing kind," from the foundry workers toiling at their
mechanical reproductions, to the scholars who labor singly to
straighten what is contorted in human "letters," to Mrs. Jones
idling in the alley. The odd humor[18] that suggests to Woolf
the possibility of adapting liturgical forms to the novel's more
secular devotions may also account for the somewhat antiquated
diction of the passage, notably in her conspicuous use of the
word "toil" to describe the work of turning out mass-produced
articles like pots. In writing about divine rather than human dis-
pensations, Woolf avoids the word "labor," with its unhappy reminder of the contentious world of political economy where cap-
ital and labor are never on easy terms. Toil, with its alternate
meaning of weave, evokes a less industrialized world of piece-
work, crafts, and guilds.

Woolf playfully elaborates here the aesthetic she first articulated
in *Mrs. Dalloway,* by which meaning is built up, like Rezia's sewing, first one thing and then another (MD, 158). Such images,
quaint as they appear in the industrialized world of giant mills
and foundries, offer modest but real instances of unalienated labor
in whose products we still can see the distinct imprint of the artist's hand. Many commentators have noted and praised the richly
detailed and democratic weave that results from Woolf's humble
aesthetic in which no one person or thing necessarily takes prece-

dence over another. Still, we should take note of any pronounced irregularities in the textual weave. They provide verbal as well as visible traces of Woolf's determination to work the idiosyncratic category, like this one about munchers and chewers, into her narrative fabric. Such irregularities are signs of authorial generosity as well as caprice; they hold the promise that anything or anyone, even Mrs. Jones idling in the alley, might eventually be accommodated in the community envisioned by the "capricious" novelistic mind. Indeed Woolf's predilection for waifs and strays ensures that the "We" she hopes to invoke in her fictions will not, in the end, consist, like the royal or editorial we, of a plurality of one, but will resound with the voice of multitudes, of plebeian as well as patrician life.

This sounds all very egalitarian and admirably selfless. Yet there are private risks as well as public benefits in rejecting the authorial "I" and embracing an all-encompassing, itinerant "we." Woolf herself was constantly aware of them, as Gillian Beer has shrewdly noted:

> "We" is an elastic pronoun, stretching in numbers and through time. Its population ranges from the exclusive pair of lovers, now, to the whole past of human history. It can welcome or rebuff the hearer. It can also colonise. Virginia Woof saw clearly that "we" may be coercive and treacherous. It invites in the individual, the subset, the excluded, who once inside may find themselves vanished with an alien group claiming on their behalf things of no benefit or relevance to themselves.[19]

Beer primarily has in mind the coercive force of the patriotic "we" or the "we" complacently adopted by "male writers to speak in universals which cover (in many senses) the experience also of women."[20] But just as menacing is the "we" that is the outcome of many years of thinking in common. Necessary and admirable as it is to find a common language that transcends the parochial identifications of gender, class, and nation, such language may leave the solitary soul, "the thing . . . that mattered" (MD, 202), without a language of its own, stranded and bereft in the land of soliloquy.

Woolf understood that the nominative "I" was as elastic, if less crowded, a pronoun as "we." It certainly was more capable of registering the more nuanced psychological states that were in danger of being overrun or obliterated by the conforming voice of the multitude. She could lambast, as she does in *A Room of One's Own*, the sterile egotism perpetuated by the male mantra "I, I, I" without underestimating the intrinsic fragility of the first-person singular. Reading her, we can often see the "I" breaking up before us on the page, most spectacularly in the language of Septimus Smith, the mad visionary of *Mrs. Dalloway*. But his pathology represents a special case, symptomatic as it is of the trauma inflicted by the Great War and of the burden of prophecy itself, to which Septimus alludes in remonstrating with "the unseen" voice summoning him "to renew society," protesting that "he did not want it . . . putting from him with a wave of his hand that eternal suffering, that eternal loneliness" (MD, 27).

Less sensational, but equally unnerving, are Woolf's representations of identity decomposing on the very threshold of nonbeing. Witness, in *The Years*, the distress of the dying Mrs. Pargiter on awaking from a fretful sleep:

"Where am I?" she cried. She was frightened and bewildered, as she often was on waking. She raised her hand; she seemed to appeal for help. "Where am I" she replied. For moment Delia was bewildered too. Where was she?
"Here, Mama! Here!" she said wildly. "Here, in your own room." (Y, 23)

Mrs. Pargiter's speech functions here as a tepid form of echolocation. She weakly emits words in order to determine, by the way they rebound, the material perimeters of her world, now drastically contracted to a deathbed.

The principle of echolocation, once established, gathers force and adherents, as we see when Delia is momentarily caught up in the general bewilderment of the phrase "Where am I?" Later she will pick up the burden of this refrain when, relieved from her deathwatch by an attending nurse, she finds herself outside the close confines of the sickroom:

Where am I? she asked herself, staring at a white jug stained pink by the setting sun. For a moment she seemed to be in some borderland between life and death. Where am I? she repeated, looking at the pink jug, for it all looked strange. Then she heard water rushing and feet thudding on the floor above. (Y, 25)

In such jarring moments of dissociated perception, objects begin to shed their customary aspect. Words no longer serve as names for things, indicators of reality. They assume a contrary, frightening power to defamiliarize the ordinary world we had (erroneously) thought thoroughly tamed by habit and the rule of reason.

The comic-grotesque way Delia reenters reality, summoned by the rush of water and thud of feet presumably coming from the water closet upstairs, enhances rather than diffuses the trance-like states when the self seems adrift in a world suddenly grown strange.

Never does the interplay between the rippled surface of Woolf's narrative syntax, in which the ventriloquizing narrator navigates nimbly from mind to mind, fact to associated fact, and the "deep structure" of her narrative grammar attain more subtle counter-point than in the opening of her last novel, *Between the Acts.* We know that there is an author present and presumably available to us, since the novel begins on a matter-of-fact, even banal note: "It was a summer's night and they were talking, in the big room with the window open to the garden, about the cesspool." The discrepancy between the natural beauty of the novel's setting and the coarse matter under discussion is reinforced by the narrator's mordant description of one conversant, a Mrs. Haines, as "a goose-faced woman with eyes protruding as if they saw something to gobble in the gutter." The mirror the narrator is holding up to human nature initially exhibits the ungainly reflection of Mrs. Haines's goose-faced countenance. It is the same mirror—"malicious; observant; expectant; expository"—as the broken mirror held up in the last act of the pageant to capture the "reality" of "present day" (BA, 186). By 1939, we thus are prompted to conjecture, modern fiction no longer could represent life as a "luminous halo, a semi-transparent envelope surrounding us from the beginning of consciousness to the end."[21] That vision of human possibility belongs to 1919. To the observant and expository author of 1939, reality—in this instance, the character of Mrs. Haines—takes the form of malicious yet not inaccurate caricature. Mrs. Haines's goose-face is as much a moral fact as her unseemly proclivity to "gobble in the gutter."

The broken, jagged tune that provides the disconcerting musical accompaniment to the pageant's final act only reinforces satire's impertinent cackle: "What a cackle, a cacophony! Nothing ended. So abrupt. And corrupt. Such an outrage; such an insult. And not plain. Very up to date, all the same. What is her game?" (BA, 183). "We," the audience that the ventriloquizer purports to speak for as well as to, is here, rather generously I think, given a chance to blurt out its objections to what is neither plain nor complimentary, yet admittedly "up to date all the same." "We" are allowed to complain about the incompleteness and the abruptness of modern art, protest against its focus on the litter, "the orts, scraps and fragments" of reality rather than on luminous and enveloping wholes.

Such passages confirm how committed Woolf remained to the realist ethics propounded in *To the Lighthouse*. She remained faithful to the last in her reporting of "facts uncompromising," which, as *To the Lighthouse* advises, have little regard for common feelings. But Woolf was equally determined to counter the sharp, incisive tongue of an observant, arguably malicious modernism with her own visionary utterances. To respond and oppose the fractious language of the present time, she devised a language released from the duties of exposition, a language capable of translating the real into a sphere where it is no longer subject to the contaminations of the transient and splintered moment. The dialogue between these two languages, the ventriloquist tethered to the present, the soliloquist anchored in the timeless medium of her own sensations and imaginings, is as much a part of the "action" in a novel by Virginia Woolf as the giving of a party, the leap from a window, the journey to a lighthouse, or the putting on a of a pageant.

Their dialogue is intermittent and is usually initiated by an unforeseen distraction or interruption, as occurs at the beginning of *Between the Acts.* The opening mood abruptly changes when a bird interrupts the human chatter the narrator has been busy recording: "A bird chuckled outside. 'A nightingale?' asked Mrs. Haines. No, nightingales didn't come so far north. It was a daylight bird chuckling, over the substance and succulence of the day, over worms, snails, grit, even in sleep" (BA, 3). The narrator presumably knows the difference between a chirp and a chuckle but is availing herself of the novelist's license to render nonhuman life anthropomorphically, just as a few moments before she had exposed the animal voracity lurking in Mrs. Haines's famished-seeming eyes. Mrs. Haines wonders if the bird sound she hears belongs to the nightingale, arguably the most poetic of birds, as Woolf herself noted in the first typescript of the novel, describing the nightingale as "the amorous, the expressive."[22] Another voice, this one unidentified, but still belonging to a character within the novel, replies with something akin to a naturalist's certainty that nightingales don't migrate so far north. Then still another voice intervenes, a voice unlike all the others we have heard, a voice that belongs to no one and is situated nowhere that we readers can discern, not even by echolocation. Presumably we are hearing the voice of the narrator, but the narrator no longer speaking as a narrator but, as it were, to herself. The word "succulence" marks off this sentence as decidedly different from the banal talk into which it makes its surprising, somewhat obtrusive appearance. Succulence is a poetic word; there is nothing conversational about it. Even if a bird could speak, we would hardly expect it to exhibit a gourmet's appreciation for the savoriness of worms and grit. Woolf rightly edited out the editorial comment in the original draft that would have made clear that the dream belonged to a bird. Either the bird-dream or the word succulence had to go. Predictably, impracticably perhaps, the word won out.

Even in such minimal acts of authorship, we can see how much Woolf added to her representations by suspending us in incertitude. Editing generally works to clarify the action or sense; here the revised and final version makes matters less clear. This revision is in keeping with Woolf's growing determination to resist saying "I am this or I am that," thus granting the authorial self more latitude, but also potentially making it more isolated from its kind, more unsure that its impressions will hold good for others. Woolf's resolve to represent the world from the point of view of incertitude gives her sentences their distinctive character. A crisis of confidence lurks at the edge of every Woolfian sentence, begetting the suspense we feel in following her sinuous sentences through the many detours, self-interruptions, and self-questionings that threaten to derail her thought and her narrative altogether. It accounts for the relief that is ours when internal doubts and external distractions are overcome, when the disparate emotions that often contend for place and primacy in the entanglements of her syntax are eventually sorted out and the sentence, often as riddled with parentheses and dashes and semicolons as it is riven with emotional division, finally completes itself. Here the uncertainty attaches to the fate of the narrative voice itself, which seems in danger of disappearing altogether into the dreamscapes of the musing mind where cesspools metamorphose easily, thanks to the unopposable logic of dreams, into succulent avian repasts.

Silence

As these examples suggest, Woolf did not so much violate as tamper with the narrative grammar of persons, by which the narrating "I" who reports and records remains separate from, if commendably responsive to, the voice both of individual characters and of public opinion. No writer of English fiction, with the possible exception of D. H. Lawrence, was more versatile in experimenting with the lyric potentials of narration, by which the subjective voice speaks without any distinct hope, often without even real desire, that its language will be heard, much less understood, by an audience. This is the distressing possibility entertained by Lily Briscoe when she thinks to herself that her paintings will be hung in attics; this is the actual hope of the playwright LaTrobe who frets that "Reality [is] too strong" for her audience and dreams of writing "a play without an audience, *the* play" (BA, 180).

Voice, however, is a more gregarious, less solitary faculty than vision—language, unlike paint, belongs to everyone and is more deeply connected to our nature as social beings, longing to communicate. To think of the unseen painting is one thing; to contemplate the unheard voice or unread page or unattended play is to approach a disassociated state of consciousness akin to autism. Woolf presents us with an icon for such autistic art in *Between the Acts* in the picture of a lady that hangs beside a portrait of a garrulous ancestor opposite the window in the dining room in Pointz Hall:

He was a talk producer, that ancestor. But the lady was a picture. In her yellow robe, leaning, with a pillar to support

her, a silver arrow in her hand, and a feather in her hair, she
led the eye up, down, from the curve to the straight, through
glades of greenery and shades of silver, dun and rose into
silence. The room was empty.

Empty, empty, empty; silent, silent, silent. The room was
a shell, singing of what was before time was; a vase stood in
the heart of the house alabaster, smooth, cold, holding the
still, distilled essence of emptiness, silence. (BA, 36–37)

It is hard to determine, after we have followed the lady garbed in
yellow "through" the looking glass presented in and by this picture, whether the empty room at journey's end is inside or outside
the picture. A tomblike quiet overcomes the narrative; nothing
resounds within this silent interior except the verbal echo of "still"
in "distilled," an echo that gives the "essence" of silence an auditory, if not material, density, as heavy, let us say, as antimatter is
purported to be. This internal echo helps dispel the stupefying
effect of the incantatory repetition "empty, empty, empty, silent,
silent, silent." The silence condensed and deposited in this shell
of a room is a silence that preexisted the Creation, originating
before time and space. It may even be a Silence that prefigures the
emptiness awaiting at the other side of time, when the universe
as we know it will have been extinguished.

The soliloquist's dream of abiding, like Mr. Ramsay, in "some
moon country uninhabited by men" is here realized in its purest
yet most dreadfully inhuman form. In the section marked *Silence*
in the earlier typescript of *Pointz Hall,* Woolf interrogates the
nameless visionary presence who seeks such a silent world: "Who
noted the silence, the emptiness? What name is to be given to the
presence which notes that a room is empty? This presence requires

a name for without a name what has an existence? And how can silence or emptiness be noted by that which has no existence . . . ?"[23] The observant presence here is not a ghost, for even a ghost may be said to have had an existence. Only a name confers existence, and the Woolf who promoted the writerly ideology of anonymity here reached a cul-de-sac, trapped in the vacant antechamber of narrative being.

This was not always the case. Woolf's fascination with silence links the beginning of her writing with its end, but at first, this fascination was confined to the traditionally novelistic sphere of human rather than primordial nature. By revisiting her beginning, we can better assess what she was either forced or willing to relinquish to attain this nameless presence. She had proclaimed in her first novel, *The Voyage Out,* a desire to write about "Silence . . . the things people don't say."[24] "Just consider," proclaims the aspiring novelist Ralph Hewit,

> it's the beginning of the twentieth century, and until a few years ago no woman had ever come out by herself and said things at all. There it was going on in the background, for all those thousands of years, this curious silent unrepresented life. Of course we're always writing about women— abusing them, or jeering at them, or worshiping them; but it's never come from women themselves. I believe we still don't know in the least how they live, or what they feel, or what they do precisely. (VO, 245)

The absolute importance of excavating the hidden, unexpressed life of women is now a commonplace of feminist criticism, although we may still marvel at the exacting standard Woolf establishes through that adverb "precisely," with its demand for the unmitigated and factual truth. Finding a language precise as well as voluble enough to express what has been consigned to silence by the "horrible domestic tradition," by the internalized codes imposed by chastity, by "the entire tea-table training" inculcated at Hyde Park Gate, was to preoccupy her for a lifetime.[25]

It had to be, inescapably, the language of indoors. The language of interiors is the language of modernism, as Woolf signaled when she had her transhistorical (as well as transsexual) heroine, Orlando, usher in the twentieth century by going indoors. Her gesture symbolizes the inward turn of narrative that Woolf greeted in such landmark essays as "Modern Fiction" and "Mr. Bennett and Mrs. Brown." It also signified Orlando's felt need, as a woman writer, to retreat into "a room of one's own," the autonomous space where a woman might speak without fear of censure, where she might harness for public and artistic ends the "complex force of femininity" silently lavished on interiors:

> For women have sat indoors all these millions of years, so that by this time the very walls are permeated by their creative force, which has, indeed so overcharged the capacity of bricks and mortar that it must needs harness itself to pens and brushes and business and politics. But this creative power differs greatly from the creative power of men. And we must conclude that it would be a thousand pities if it were hindered or wasted, for it was won by centuries of the most drastic discipline, and there is nothing to take its place. It would be a thousand pities if women wrote like men, or lived like men, or looked like men.[26]

Woolf's respect for the drastic discipline that is the woman writer's most conspicuous inheritance from her creative female forbears underlies her conviction that a woman's language, shaped in confinement, allows her "to say a great many things which would be inaudible if one marched straight up and spoke out."[27]

Yet we can also detect in her writing a growing restlessness with such prolonged imaginative confinement, a restlessness that surfaces, for example, in the exuberant opening of *Mrs. Dalloway*, the novel in which Woolf's modernity and her heroine make exhilarating contact with the out-of-doors:

> What a lark! What a plunge! For so it had always seemed to her when, with a little squeak of the hinges, which she could hear now, she had burst open the French windows and plunged at Bourton into the open air. How fresh, how calm, stiller than this of course, the air was in the early morning; like the flap of a wave; the kiss of a wave; chill and sharp and yet (for a girl of eighteen as she then was) solemn, feeling as she did, standing there at the open window, that something awful was about to happen; . . . (MD, 3)

A profusion of parentheses, exclamation points and semicolons at once reflect and subdue the manic gaiety of this verbal and existential plunge into the open air. Woolf's singular, strategic use of the semicolon will become a habitual, indeed symptomatic, feature of her prose. By its aid, she is able to regulate the excited rush of perceptions that threaten to outrun her powers of expression. Yet such syntactically and typographically elaborate sentences may also represent an anxiety formation, a linguistic calmative to subdue the agoraphobia instilled by all those years of confinement indoors. Perhaps this explains the heroine's ominous premonition that something awful was about to happen, and the inordinately heavy time symbolism of the novel that is always reminding us, not just Mrs. Dalloway, of the "leaden" tolling of the bells.

A similar dread overcomes Mrs. Ramsay in *To the Lighthouse* when, in the midst of her domestic crooning, she is suddenly roused by an unidentifiable rustle of wind or burst of sound that "like some ghostly roll of drums remorselessly beat the measure of life" (TTL, 20). The rhythm of a Woolfian sentence is calculated to counter the monotony of this remorseless beat by which life measures and doles out life. Words fashioned to counter that rhythm can even turn failure into an opportunity for a human success (however impermanent). If you doubt the power of words to accomplish so much, consider this exchange, when Mr. Ramsay, nearly speechless with anxiety, demands comfort from his wife:

> He was a failure, he repeated. Well, look then, feel then. Flashing her needles, glancing round about her, out of the window, into the room, at James himself, she assured him, beyond a shadow of a doubt, by her laugh, her poise, her competence (as a nurse carrying a light across a dark room assures a fractious child) that it was real; the house full; the garden blowing. (TTL, 41)

This intimate exchange between husband and wife is played out in silence. Indeed the entire passage describes the intense desire to obliterate a word—failure—into which the entire misery and persistent anxiety of Mr. Ramsay's existence has been condensed.

It is by outward signs, the language of gesture, that Mrs. Ramsay communicates her own inward agitation as she prepares to reply to this mute appeal. The flashing needles communicate their point and fire to the glance she darts impatiently, a little wildly, out of the window. Her gaze then returns indoors, back to James. Her silent glance traces an entire circuit of relations between what lies outside and beyond the window (where we might glimpse how the sea is eating up the very ground we stand on) and the room in which the entire complex force of femininity has asserted itself. Yet we should also notice that there seems to be a third silent participant in this complex interchange. Who is it, after all, who commands, "Well, look then, feel then." To whom are these words directed? All we can know for certain is that the imperative to look and to feel must be obeyed. Even the words on the page seem to obey it. The agitated language that captures the flash and flow of charged glances eventually subsides; the "sentence" recovers its composure and pronounces, in a serene and stately measure, the humanly enabling conviction that "it was real."

Whatever the uncertainties and indeterminacies that plague Woolf's sentences, they work to provide the best possible assurance anyone can receive—the assurance of reality. Such assurances, by their nature, can only be temporary. They seldom come in the forms nor in the manner we expect. But the making of them is the primary burden of the language of Virginia Woolf. These assurances constitute her finest work in her life as an author.

5

The Critic

THE DEMON OF READING AT WORK

You might think that Woolf the author and Woolf the critic would work hand in hand in revolutionizing the way the novel is written and the way it is read. How logical as well as untroubled a relationship it promises to be: the critic explaining and advocating the work of the author, the author confirming the insights of the critic; the author working to deepen, extend, and confirm our sense of reality, the critic working to sort out the good, true, and enduring from the bad, false, and ephemeral.

But the relationship between Woolf the author and Woolf the critic was not always so harmonious or so emotionally tidy. They had less in common than one might suppose. Whereas Woolf the novelist impersonalizes herself with such discipline and determination that even her soliloquies seem at times as if they were uttered by some unembodied consciousness, Woolf the critic is a more substantial personality who betrays no immediate plans to purge herself of all the biases, impurities, caprices, and contradictions that adulterate her opinions.

Indeed, never was the demon of reading more active and more visible than in Woolf's life as a critic. The unruly voice that whispers I hate, I love, is never hushed in her critical essays but is allowed to express itself whenever and however it wants. As a result, you will never have a better opportunity to get to know Woolf as a literary personality than by reading her criticism, since there she exposes her personal disposition, her likes and dislikes, most candidly and unapologetically to public view.

The critical personality Woolf displays is (at least to me) quite appealing, but, as always with Woolf, it is not as consistent or even as transparent as we might like or expect. We know, for instance, the critics she admired. She is unstinting and unreserved in her praise of

the downright vigour of a Dryden, or Keats with his fine and natural bearing, his profound insight and sanity, or Flaubert and the tremendous power of his fanaticism, or Coleridge . . . , brewing in his head the whole of poetry and letting issue now and then one of those profound general statements which are caught up by the mind when hot with the friction of reading as if they were of the soul of the book itself.[1]

Yet what she valued in these critics was not only peculiar to them but perhaps unsuited to her. Thus she could admire them without feeling the desire to imitate or follow their example. She does not attempt to rival Dryden's vigor or impersonate Keats's fine bearing (at least not for very long); she seems positively anxious not to appear a fanatic of Flaubertian intensity, knowing that she had trouble enough in disarming the doubts and defenses of readers already suspicious of a woman writing, and writing from a feminist slant at that.

Only Coleridge returns time and again to urge her, often against her own inclinations, to formulate more impersonal and disinterested judgments. Coleridge, indeed, was for her, as for T. S. Eliot, perhaps the greatest, certainly the *purest* of critics, a distinction Woolf conferred on him for his "indifference to, in his hatred of, 'mere personality.' " Although she could affirm, with Coleridge, that affections may be the "best part of humanity," she nonetheless insisted that the pure critic mounts "into an atmosphere where the substance of [human] desires has been shredded by infinite refinements and discriminations of all its grossness" and the light of criticism "is concentrated and confined in one ray—in the art itself."[2]

By such standards, Woolf does not rate highly as a "pure" critic of literature. Her criticism, as we have already seen, was of the grosser sort—adulterated by personal likings or aversions, alloyed by doubts, hesitations, and outright perplexities. She was so intent on tracking "the flight of the mind" in all its unpredictable coursings that to capture the soul of the book was an outcome that, however devoutly wished, was never confidently expected: "The critic may be able to abstract the essence and feast upon it undisturbed, but for the rest of us in every book there is something— sex, character, temperament—which, as in life, rouses affection or repulsion; and, as in life, sways and prejudices; and again, as in life, is hardly to be analysed by the reason."[3]

The rest of us presumably belong to the tribe that Woolf, after Dr. Johnson, identified as the common reader. The common reader, a being quite distinct in her mind from the mass audience, is the presiding spirit and dedicatee of her first collection of essays, whose early working title was simply "Reading." *The Common Reader* was originally to have contained an introductory chapter entitled "Byron and Mr Briggs" that offered a portrait of the character and opinions of Mr. Briggs, a figure Woolf invented to represent the habits and judgments of the common reader. Mr. Briggs, as she portrayed him, could be ruled by "unguided passion . . . capable of doing enormous harm as a glance at [contemporary] literature [is bound to] prove," yet his passion is admirably "voluntary and individual," even "lawless."[4] He is a person of discriminating, not socially conditioned tastes. He is person who acts, or rather reads, according to the promptings of two instincts Woolf believed were "deeply implanted in our souls—the instinct to complete; the instinct to judge."[5] Like Johnson, Woolf rejoiced to concur with the common reader, whose judgments, however prejudiced by feeling or marred by ignorance, ultimately supersede, so Johnson insisted, "all the refinements of subtlety and dogmatism of learning."

Woolf's respect for the untutored but reliable judgment of the common reader went deeper than Johnson's, however, and formed the core of her identity as a critic. It irradiates her vision of tradition as deeply embedded in the common life. It attracts her to the dim shades where the "lives of the obscure" are huddled together, silenced by the remorseless rule of history that consigns the inarticulate to oblivion unless the ventriloquizing historian or critic bestows upon them "the divine relief of communication."[6] A pure critic, focused on the work of art and not on the circumstances in which it came to be written, would be immune to such fascinations. "A student of letters," Woolf not unreasonably objected, is so much in the habit of striding through the centuries from one pinnacle to the next that he forgets all the hubbub that once surged round the base; how Keats lived in a street and had a neighbor and his neighbor a family—the rings widen infinitely; how Oxford Street ran turbulent with men and women while De Quincey walked with Ann. And such considerations are not trivial if only because they had their effect upon things that we are wont to look upon as isolated births, and to judge, therefore, in a spirit that is more than necessarily dry.[7]

Tradition did not suggest to Woolf, as it famously did to T. S. Eliot, a majestic panorama of sublime pinnacles spread out over time in a simultaneous and relatively uniform order, a panorama continually renewed and altered by the successive works of individual talents. Tradition encompasses the wide, undifferentiated expanses that lie between and lead up to the summits; it is enlivened by all the hubbub at its base.

To symbolically register this belief, Woolf places the four sketches that compose "The Lives of the Obscure" at the very center of the first *Common Reader*. We know this is not an accidental placement, given how carefully Woolf considered the historical and thematic relation of essays in ordering the collection, which begins with "The Pastons and Chaucer" and concludes with "How It Strikes a Contemporary." No history, she suggests, is complete without consulting the "faded, out-of-date, obsolete library" where "the obscure sleep . . . slouching against each other as if they were too drowsy to stand upright." Moreover, Woolf noted that there is, as a personal inducement, the special romance of feeling oneself "a deliverer advancing with lights across the waste of years to the rescue of some stranded ghost."[8] Woolf's ideal literary, indeed human, history would satisfy the gossip's curiosity about the changing fortunes of individuals, families, and communities, the annalist's interest in the social and cultural data of everyday life, and the historian's fascination with epochal events—like the exploration of the new world or the writing of Shakespeare's plays and Montaigne's essays.

Woolf's forays beyond the patrolled, well-illuminated grounds maintained by the custodians of literary culture provide us brief but revelatory glimpses of those now overgrown trails where little-known writers once struggled toward Parnassus. Along those seldom visited byways, Woolf insists, we might see the original seed-beds of the common language and conventions that great artists later put to lasting use. Still, those wishing to follow in her footsteps may find it hard going, for what she offers us is an approach, not a set itinerary. Woolf's criticism is in many ways the criticism of a novelist, reflecting as it does the novelist's congenital distrust of systems. "Reading at Random," the first title proposed for the essay she was working on at the time of her death, proclaims her belief that the mind's spontaneous interest, rather than any prescribed method, should dictate what and how we read. "In literary criticism at least," she elsewhere asserted, "the wish to attain completeness is more often than not a will o' the wisp which lures one past the occasional ideas which may perhaps have truth in them towards an unreal symmetry which has none."[9] Her conviction that truth is more likely to show itself in the unmolested part rather than in the fabricated whole disinclines her to attempt prescriptive criticism in the more dogmatic manner of T. S. Eliot or F. R. Leavis. Although she does not hesitate to offer advice in "How Should One Read a Book?," she stresses the interrogation at the end of the title and warns us in her opening remarks that "Even if I could answer the question for myself, the answer would apply only to me and not to you." Woolf comes as close to an unqualified libertarian line in this essay as she ever does in insisting that no law or authority must be permitted to fetter the freedom of reading: "Everywhere else we may be bound by law and convention—there we have none."[10] We should not expect strict teachings from the critic who writes to demonstrate such a belief, nor hope for the logical instruction exemplified in I. A. Richards's *Practical Criticism*, with its protocols for reading.

Woolf sought to give us what she felt no critics ever give—"full weight to the desire of the mind for change."[11] Such, at least, was the desire of her own mind, and she did not scruple to please herself. Her best essays nimbly juggle the throng of contradictory but dependably fertile suggestions her mind tosses up while reading until it settles, in the pensive aftermath of her mental exertions, upon the final impression left hovering in the mind like a mote momentarily irradiated by light. It is at this quiet but critical moment that reading elides into criticism; it is then that it is possible "to continue reading without the book before you, to hold one shadow-shape against another."[12] In this second stage, the contrary emotions aroused in reading are reconciled and rationally composed into a literary judgment.

There are, however, distinct limitations, even dangers, in always consulting your own mind, and Woolf acknowledges them in "Phases of Fiction," her testimonial to the rewards and insights that accrue to reading at random. Reading takes us into a world "as inhabitable as the real world," but "such a world, it may be urged against it, is always in process of creation. Such a world, it may be added, likewise against it, is . . . a world created in obedience to tastes that may be peculiar to one temperament and distasteful to another," so that any record of reading "is bound to be limited, personal, erratic."[13]

Woolf's literary opinions, then, are best understood, and their value most accurately assessed, when we recognize that she speaks less as a critic of supreme and learned authority than as a common reader of strong feeling and pronounced tastes. Never could it be said of Woolf what she said of Hazlitt: "He is one of the rare critics who have thought so much that they can dispense with reading."[14] For Woolf, everything could be dispensed with *but* reading. The etymologies of these crucial terms—criticism and reading—may help clarify the distinction I propose. Criticism derives from the same verbal root as crisis: the Greek *krinein*, to discern, to separate. If we recall this etymology, we can appreciate that to speak even loosely of a *critical* judgment is to employ a loaded figure of speech. Any authentic critical pronouncement has the power to involve us in a moment of intellectual and moral crisis that reflects, and indeed requires, absolute rather than qualified judgments. The genuine critic performs an act of radical separation, dividing the good from the not so good or from the distinctly bad. Woolf is thinking of criticism in this sense when she laments that the modern world lacks the great critic—the Dryden, the Johnson, the Coleridge, the Arnold—whom "if you had taken to him some eccentricity of the moment, would have brought it into touch with permanence and tethered it by his own authority in the contrary blasts of praise and blame."[15] To read is also a word whose historic meanings extend into its modern usages. Reading traces its roots to *reden*, to explain, and *raeden*, to counsel, thus establishing common ground between the work of interpretation and the imparting of wisdom.

Woolf is more likely to offer us the counsel derived from reading than report the determinate findings of "pure" criticism. Accordingly, her critical idiom is not rich in abstract concepts like "objective correlative," "dissociation of sensibility," epiphany, or "the phantom aesthetic state" that epitomize the modern genius for objectifying subjective states and analyzing aesthetic effects. Her critical legacy consists rather in an image-repertoire rich in symbolic formations: a room of one's own, the androgynous mind, the leaning tower, granite and rainbow. Because of Woolf we now appreciate not only the monetary significance, but, more crucially, the symbolic import of five hundred pounds and three guineas in underwriting the creative life and preserving the intellectual independence of women in a society where culture is bought and paid for. If Woolf survives as a true critic, as she herself would define one—a reader who possesses "the power of seeming to bring to light what was already there beforehand, instead of imposing anything from the outside"[16]—she will do so by virtue of her own necromantic powers to revive the neglected or underestimated ancestors of our literary heritage: the revered "common reader," reinvested with the authority Johnson ascribed to him as the final arbiter of all claims to poetical honors; the dreaded Angel of the House, that wraithlike spirit of devotion, self-sacrifice, and submission who haunted the moral being of Victorian women,[17] and the Angel's vampiric double, Milton's bogey,[18] a "large and imposing figure of a gentleman" interposed between women's imagination and "a view of the open sky" who effectively "shut[s] out the view."[19] Woolf summons these ideological phantoms from the shadows so that they may be exorcised once and for all, thus freeing the woman writer to describe her body, depict her life, criticize her society, or simply gaze at the heavens. These are all

considerable achievements, but surely nothing rivals the emotional drama and ideological importance of Woolf's *coup de thé-
âtre*—the resurrection of Shakespeare's sister, restored to her name
(Judith) and provided with a biography typifying the historical
plight of any woman with talent, even genius, but lacking money
and education, who was schooled only in the repressive codes of
chastity, altruism, and anonymity, who was in fact "so thwarted
and hindered by other people, so tortured and pulled asunder by
her own contrary instincts, that she must have lost her health and
sanity to a certainty."[20]

Unmethodical Methods

Woolf might have argued in defense of her unorthodox, antino-
mian and irregular "methods" that the times made more orthodox
methods virtually impossible. "The scattered dinner-tables of the
modern world, the chase and eddy of the various currents which
compose society of our time," she maintained, "could only be
dominated by a giant of fabulous dimensions."[21] Though she
shared the common reader's suspicions of "fixed labels and settled
hierarchies," she was somewhat dazed, as both novelist and re-
viewer-critic, by the breakup of the reading public into a "bewildering variety" of audiences: "the daily Press, the weekly Press,
the monthly Press; the English public and the American public;
the best-seller public and the worst-seller public; the high-brow
public and the red-blood public, all now organized self-conscious
entities capable through their various mouthpieces of making
their needs known and their approval or displeasure felt."[22] The
reading public had become the reading publics, with different

rather than converging interests, and Woolf was by no means convinced that reviewers, through whose ranks she first joined the literary estate, eased the confusion and contention among them. Her pamphlet "Reviewing" (1939), which provoked Leonard Woolf into appending a dissenting note, contains the startling suggestion that reviewers abolish themselves as a class and resurrect themselves as consultants, expositors, or expounders, that is, as self-interested readers.[23]

For her part, Woolf assumed the position and persona of the outsider without a personal stake either in established hierarchies or in the periodic agitations of the marketplace; an outsider, of course who, as the daughter of Leslie Stephen and an accomplished and esteemed author in her own right, had an insider's experience of the workings, as well as the singular personalities, of the literary world. To present herself as a common reader and literary outsider was not, however, as disingenuous as might first appear. As an aspiring woman novelist who lacked a formal education, a fact she exploits with sharp humor in the opening pages of *A Room of One's Own,* she may have had no real choice in adopting such a strategy.

Nevertheless, assuming the place of an outsider served her well, or, which is not quite the same thing, she made the most of her outsider status. Woolf was one of the first critics to demonstrate to us the special authority and unique advantages of those standing outside of or at the periphery of those centers where social and cultural power are concentrated. She exploited an exclusion that had been imposed until it begins to appear an exclusion she had *chosen.* This strategy allows her to develop larger, impartial, less compromised views. Woolf became more and more confident exercising the outsider's privilege; we can feel her critical posture stiffening into less submissive attitudes as she moves from the generally disarming polemic of *A Room of One's Own* to the more aloof, even strident *Three Guineas*. Eventually she was to fashion something like a cult around an outsider who was the object of a lifelong fascination—the itinerant figure of Anon, the nameless village poet, sometimes man, sometimes woman, who, though despised by master and mistress of the Manor and feared when not hated by the elders of the Church, enjoyed "the outsider's privilege to mock the solemn, to comment upon the established."[24]

As an outsider possessed of "inside information," Woolf commands, however, an authority of a peculiar sort. It is authority predicated on the virtual incontrovertibility of what Gertrude Stein called "personal knowledge." In "What Is English Literature," Stein proposes a distinction between two ways of thinking about English literature, "the literature as it is a history of it and the literature as it is a history of you."[25] Stein and Woolf both wrote of literature as a "history of you," that is, as primarily a history of reading: "Any one of us and anyway those of us that have always had the habit of reading have our own history of English literature inside us, the history as by reading we have come to know it."[26] The facts and events that constitute the historian's "history of it," which Stein, in her inimitable way, firmly dismisses as "none of my business," Woolf, too, firmly if politely, repudiates in offering her own distinction, less eccentric but ultimately more drastic than Stein's, between the common reader and the professional scholar who objectifies literature as a "history of it."

Stein seems content in keeping her knowledge inside her, telling us what she indisputably does know, which anyone, or at least anyone with the habit of reading, can see for herself. In Woolf the history of reading as we have come to know it is at once demysti-

fied and dramatized. She is our finest dramatist of what would
seem a singularly unpromising subject—our silent relations with
books. She analyzes this relation through all its tortuous phases,
beginning with initial reactions, following up on passing thoughts
and irresistible digressions, and concluding with the ordered ideas
and the judgments, however provisional, with which reading
ought to conclude. She does not immediately appeal, as Stein
does, to what we know, what is inside us and in a sense remains
there, open to periodic inspection. Instead she tries to recapture
the personal experience of a book or poem by re-creating the scene
in which her reading took place. Typically she tells us how she
settled into a niche close to a window where "somehow or another, the windows being open, and the book held so that it rested
upon a background of escallonia hedges and distant blue, instead
of being a book it seemed as if what I read was laid upon the
landscape not printed, bound, or sewn up, but somehow the
product of trees and fields and the hot summer sky, like the air
which swam, on fine mornings, round the outlines of things."[27]

Woolf habitually measures what she reads against such vistas.
The window may open out onto a complementary scene of
human labor, disclose a patch of uncultivated nature, or look out
onto the wide prospect of life where the outlines of things may
be clearly and distinctly seen. I do not mean that she insists on
referring what she learns and feels in the act of reading to some
abstract but emotionally compelling idea of Nature or Society or
God that will endow a literary work with transcendent meaning
or enduring relevance. For Woolf, literature was both the mirror
and the sanctuary of reality, of things in themselves.

But she was also a formalist who believed that literature constituted its own reality—was a transmutation, not a slavish tran-

scription, of Life. As a novelist, she especially appreciated that much of life that seems so vital to those who experience it soon vanishes, losing not only its burning interest but its actual status as "the real." So much of "real life" is perishable, possessing only the fugitive interest of the topical. Great art solves this problem by putting life into conflict with something that is not life (which we identify as "form"). Thus, in an imaginary but typical example she gives in *A Room of One's Own,* as we sit reading a novel, we might feel, on the one hand that "You—John the hero—must live, or I shall be in the depths of despair. On the other, we feel, Alas John, you must die, because the shape of the book requires it."[28] In forcing this choice between what we desire and what truth demands, the novel confirms its "integrity" both as a moral record and as a work of art. The "integrity" of great art consists in holding together "all sorts of antagonist and opposed emotions" so that the reader is left with "the conviction . . . that this is the truth."[29] Nor is this conviction to be lightly dismissed as readerly solipsism, since it is Nature, Woolf contends, that has traced in invisible ink on the walls of the mind a premonition that great artists corroborate. Masterpieces (Woolf was not embarrassed by that term or by the concept of unimpeachable greatness) survive because they possess this integrity of feeling and form, because they unite Life and Form, which in lesser books are allowed to split apart or tear themselves asunder. They attain and communicate "a complete finality" that summons all our faculties in reading, so that "some consecration descends upon us from their hands which we return to life, feeling it more keenly and understanding it more deeply than before."[30]

The truth of things was not, then, to be contested, but rather to be *determined,* or more precisely, *re*determined in new acts of creation, new readings. Woolf does not hesitate to make these determinations about literary value and, without any ideological fuss, can dismiss bad writing for what it is: a revenge not against art, but against reality: "The bad writer seems to possess a predominance of the day-dreaming power, he lives all day long in that region of artificial light where every factory girl becomes a duchess, where if truth be told, most people spend a few moments every day revenging themselves upon reality. The bad books are not the mirrors but the vast distorted shadows of life; they are a refuge, a form of revenge."[31] Bad writing is bad in itself and bad for us because it contains not too much reality, but too little. Perhaps only a critic of Woolf's extensive and declared interest in noncanonical works could understand the pleasures of bad books without feeling obliged to attribute to them imaginary merits.

The wider views afforded by open windows through which the outlines of things appear in their shimmering reality may break the concentration, but that is their purpose—to provide stimulants and correctives to the absorption of reading. However sinuous her prose, Woolf is actually of a more disruptive temper than Stein, whom nothing seems to arrest as she advances her argument through the precisely modulated repetitions that eventually settle in a triumphant assertion of common and incontrovertible sense, as in the following grand definition of what is, in fact, English literature:

As I say description of the complete the entirely complete daily island life has been England's glory. Think of Chaucer, think of Jane Austen, think of Anthony Trollope, and the life of things shut up with that daily life is the poetry, think of all the lyrical poets, think what they say and what they have. They have shut in with them in their daily island life but completely shut in with them all the things that just in enumeration make poetry, and they can and do enumerate and they can and do make poetry, this enumeration. That is all one side of English literature and indeed anybody knows, where it grows, the daily life the complete daily life and the things shut in with that complete daily life.[32]

Woolf, on the other hand is the mistress of deferral, dilation, and delay. If she prides herself in being a highbrow who "rides [her mind] at a gallop across country in pursuit of an idea,"[33] she also boasts the ability to alter her course in midstride, detour an argument into unsuspected places, and so re-create the excitement, or the indignation, of arriving at a conclusion other than what one hoped to find on setting out. However much she blamed the "tea-table training" inculcated at Hyde Park Gate for the "suavity" and "politeness" she detected in her *Common Reader* essays, she put her training to unexpected and good use in devising a rhetoric that allowed her to "say a great many things which would be inaudible if one marched straight up and spoke out."[34]

We can see the benefits of this manner in the confiding first sentence of "On Not Knowing Greek," where Woolf manages to create a community of (unscholarly) opinion simply by beginning with an utterly disarming admission of shared ignorance:

For it is vain and foolish to talk of Knowing Greek, since in our ignorance we should be at the bottom of any class of schoolboys, since we do not know how the words sounded, or where precisely we ought to laugh, or how the actors acted, and between this foreign people and ourselves there is not only difference of race and tongue but a tremendous breach of tradition.[35]

Tradition is imperiled by historical ruptures, fatal ignorances, unexpected blockages. Such breaches appear insuperable, discouraging any attempts at repair, were it not for the encouragement offered by that opening "For," which reminds us that in picking up a book, whether in ignorance or in full knowledge of our subject, we are resuming a discussion or dialogue already and still under way.

This is what it means for Woolf and for the reader of Woolf to enter into a tradition—it means joining others at a point of common conjunctions. Even when Woolf's singular and strategic use of conjunctions is startlingly abrupt, they still strike the sociable note of resumed dialogue, as in the arresting opening of *A Room of One's Own*—"But you may say, we asked you to speak about women and fiction—what has that got to do with a room of one's own?" We are not eased into an argument but plunged immediately into its midst. The "but" of expostulation already sounds a note of heated, if decorous, exchange, one that promises to leave the audience at the conclusion of her talk not only informed of the social, economic, and psychological factors that affect creativity, but, equally important, instructed in the suggestive and persuasive powers of symbolic representations. Those who follow Woolf through multiple changes in identity (she speaks first in her own person, while allowing that "I" denotes a "convenient term for somebody who has no real being," then as Mary Beton, who will conduct most of the research and represent Woolf's findings, finally returning to her "real" identity as woman of letters just in time to deliver the peroration); those, as I say, who persist through all the distractions, digressions, ellipses, and interruptions that divert or retard her train of thought—but that never, such is the providence that rules Woolf's imaginative and intellectual world, derail it—will eventually learn what a room of one's own has to do with the question of women and fiction.

READING IN CRISIS

Woolf, then, might be said to have pioneered reader response criticism of a very sophisticated, if unmethodical, kind. And yet it must also be said that the author of an essay advising "How Should One Read a Book?" or a review admonishing "The Wrong Way of Reading" is already uneasily aware of some impending complication and crisis threatening the future of reading, hence the future of literature itself. Of course, to see modernity as a time of unprecedented, convulsive change was not unique to Woolf, but perhaps no modern critic put the crisis in such bold, mischievous terms as Woolf did in her famous claim that in or about December 1910 human character changed.[36] She measured these changes as a novelist might be expected to—by noting the more open character of one's cook, by suggesting that Clytemnestra and not Agamemnon would now elicit our sympathy, and by considering how the "horrible domestic tradition" condemned Jane Carlyle, woman of genius, to scouring saucepans instead of writing books. It was this change in character manifested in the altered relations between "masters and servants, husbands and wives, parents and children" that made modernity new.

It is one of history's many ironies that human character seems to have changed so radically in the eighty-odd years since Woolf made that claim that to many it has ceased to exist entirely. At best, Woolf's fascination with Mrs. Brown or "character in itself" may seem old-fashioned, a quaint fiction easily repudiated by those who no longer believe in the reality of the self, much less the moral existence of character. But Woolf cherished human character as something *achieved,* not fantasized; character was the supreme refinement of our social and cultural evolution, and prose was its greatest expositor. To read a character was to read not just a personal history, but the history of civilization as it makes its errant way through time.

Life, in fact, was not always, in Woolf's famous formulation of modern existence, a "luminous halo surrounding us from the beginning of consciousness to the end."[37] The Elizabethans, for example, did not have a sense of character in the modern understanding of that word, as one can see in comparing, as Woolf does, Annabella in "Tis Pity She's a Whore" to Anna Karenina. Anna is "flesh and blood, nerves and temperament, has heart, brain, body and mind," in other words is a full incarnation of a human being. But we will find no trace of character as we understand the word in Annabella, who "is flat and crude as a face painted on a playing card." We know very little about her, nor do we need to, since as a literary creation she "is without depth, without range, without intricacy."[38] By contrast, even the most ordinary mind of someone alive in or about 1910 would feel, on any ordinary day, that it receives "a myriad impressions—trivial, fantastic, evanescent, or engraved with the sharpness of steel," impressions that, as they accumulate and shape "themselves into the life of Monday or Tuesday," reveal how "the accent falls differently from of old."[39]

As a laconic note in her last reading notebook attests, "the modern . . . the growth of articulateness" are synonymous phenomena in Woolf's mind.

Art assists and refines the growing self-consciousness of human character by liberating "us of the enormous burden of the unexpressed."[40] This is the theme that dominates Woolf's reading of history from her *Common Reader* essays, through the brilliant feminist revisionism of *A Room of One's Own*, to her last major critical project, which gives pride of place to two figures whose role in the making of the tradition Woolf was intent on commemorating. One is Anon, "the common voice singing out of doors," who ushers us to the threshold of individuality and the print culture that memorializes the self. Without Anon's singing at the back door of the manor houses and staging his dramas in churchyards and the marketplace, the English in the silent centuries before the advent of the book "might be a dumb race, a race of merchants, soldiers, priests, who left behind them stone houses, cultivated fields and great churches, but no words."[41] The other is, of course, "The Reader," whom Woolf presents not as a bloodless and timeless personification, but as a historical being who "comes into existence some time at the end of the sixteenth century" upon the death of Anon, and whose life history "could we discover it would be worth writing, for the effect it had upon literature."[42]

The Common Reader may be regarded as the first volume of that life history. Woolf's historical starting point is in the family chronicle recounted in "The Pastons and Chaucer": Margaret Paston, the mother dutifully writing her husband "letters of an honest bailiff to his master, explaining, giving news, rendering accounts,"[43] and her son, John Paston, who escapes the country life by going to London and becoming a gentleman. His outward change is accompanied by an equally momentous inner change, evidenced in a desire, rare in the country if not to a gentleman, however newly made, to write of things that have no immediate practical import ("to crack a joke, to send a piece of gossip or to instruct . . . knowingly and even subtly, upon the conduct of a love affair").[44] Equally telling is his pleasure in reading Chaucer, whose poems were like "a mirror in which figures move brightly, silently, and compactly, showed him the very skies, fields, and people whom he knew, but rounded and complete."[45]

In the growing inwardness of John Paston's character, we may witness the shift in family and social relations that led to the birth of the reader. Woolf's account of that momentous mutation sharply contrasts with Walter Benjamin's picture of the reader stranded in the silence of unspoken words, isolated, as the listener of the storyteller's tales was not, from the rich lore of experience. In essays like "The Elizabethan Lumber Room," "Notes on an Elizabethan Play," and the drafts of "Anon," Woolf considers how the English reader developed habits in response to the customs of the playhouse. On the stage, where "people had to meet, to quip and crank, to suffer interruptions, to talk of ordinary things" the playgoer could overhear, as it were, his native language developing into a finely expressive medium that would reach perfection in Dryden.[46] But "the publicity of the stage and the perpetual presence of a second person" soon failed to satisfy a mind tired of company, a mind seeking "to think, not to act; to comment, not to share; to explore its own darkness, not the bright-lit-up surfaces of others."[47]

Such a mind belongs to the (newly born) reader. This reader will turn to Donne, Montaigne, Sir Thomas Browne, "the keepers of the keys of solitude."[48] To Montaigne alone belongs the art "of talking of oneself, following one's own vagaries, giving the whole map, weight, colour, and circumference of the soul in its confusion, its variety, its imperfection."[49] Montaigne, reading the book of himself, counsels us that "Communication is health, communication is happiness," a message the disordered mind of Septimus Smith makes the burden of his prophecy in *Mrs. Dalloway* even as he enacts the dark fate of modernity—the death of the soul.

If Montaigne is the man who "achieved at last a miraculous adjustment of all these wayward parts that constitute the human soul,"[50] Sir Thomas Browne, "the first of the autobiographers," is a character in whom "we first become conscious of impurities which hereafter stain literature with so many freakish colours that, however hard we try, it is difficult to be certain whether we are looking at a man or his writing."[51] All the writers who interest Woolf present this freakishness, this uncertainty: Donne, Defoe, Sterne, the Brontës, George Eliot, Meredith, Hardy, Henry James, Conrad, Lawrence, Proust, and Joyce, to name only those who occasioned her most brilliant commentary. As *Persuasion* attests, even Jane Austen, exemplary in her impersonality and "exquisite discrimination of human values" might, had she lived, have "devised a method, clear and composed as ever, but deeper and more suggestive, for conveying not only what people say, but what they leave unsaid; not only what they are, but what life is."[52] She would have been a forerunner not only of E. M. Forster (and, of course, Woolf herself), but of Henry James and Proust.

In coursing through literary history, Woolf the critic does not strand her reader, as Woolf the novelist stranded Orlando, in the present moment, awaiting deliverance. The literature of the future, Woolf prophesized, would revive the power of poetry to abstract and exalt feeling so that we might understand not just what we are, but what life is; it would possess the drama's power to concentrate, generalize, and heighten emotion so that we might see not Annabella in love, but love itself; would extend the empire of prose, in which both the great and trivial facts of existence, the common sensations of the mind—including its humors, the emotions aroused by music, by crowds, by certain people, or merely by the play of light against the water—would be calibrated with a precision the poets might admire.[53]

SEX AND THE FUTURE OF READING

Such a future is unthinkable and certainty will never materialize without a corresponding change in sex-consciousness, since for Woolf sex-consciousness is indistinguishable from the great problem of modernity: the mind divided against itself. Woolf's determination to include the judgments of the common reader, the lives of the obscure, and the voice of Anon (who she believes was probably a woman) in her history of English literature helped revolutionize not only the way we conceive of literary history but how we understand women's relation to the art of writing. Modern feminist criticism may be said to be a series of commentaries on Woolf's original insight that "we think back through our mothers if we are women."[54] Woolf undertakes to trace this genealogy because women, historically denied the education and the material means to qualify as unconscious inheritors of the tradition, necessarily wrote not only differently, but also less expansively and confidently than men.

These feminist concerns were not ones she grew or stumbled into; they are directly in her critical sight from the very beginning of her writing life, determining her point of view as a critic. As early as 1918, in a review of R. Brimley Johnson's *Women Novelists,* Woolf proposed that the question of women writers was "not merely one of literature, but of social history":

> What, for example, was the origin of the extraordinary outburst in the eighteenth century of novel writing by women? Why did it begin then, and not in the time of the Elizabethan renaissance? Was the motive which finally determined them to write a desire to correct the current view of their sex expressed in so many volumes and for so many ages by male writers? If so, their art is at once possessed of an element which should be absent from the work of all previous writers.[55]

Today these questions sound quite familiar, so much so that we might forget that their answers, which took Woolf a lifetime to formulate, even today are by no means definitive and, in some cases, are incomplete. We are still seeking to resolve the major issues of feminist inquiry: the social and economic conditions of creativity (or, as Woolf puts it, how to feed the artist); the relation, if any, of gender and genre, gender and literary form, the body and language.

The most stubborn, as well as most controversial issue Woolf addressed was whether it is possible to identify an element or elements of style or attitude missing in male writers that would, so it seemed reasonable to assume, mark a work as distinctly female. Motive does not seem to be a distinguishing element, for, as Woolf knew too well, the reasons why different women write are by no means consistent and uniform. Fanny Burney, "the mother of En-

glish fiction," was not inspired "by a single wish to redress a grievance," while her headstrong daughter, Charlotte Brontë, could
barely contain her anger. Woolf thought it might be more fruitful
to look at the different way men and women apportion their day.
She reasoned that the pace and tread of the woman's sentence
would reflect the daily rhythms, the fitful sequences that marked
and limited a woman's life *whatever* she may have felt about it—
happy or resentful, fulfilled or aggrieved. "For interruptions there
will always be": Women who write may never escape the fatality of
that sentence, which determines not only the way women write—
sporadically, in short, not sustained, bouts of concentration—but
the way the experiences of ordinary life enter consciousness, not
in successive waves, but in intervals snatched from supervision of
children, duty in the sitting room, attendance at the family table.

More controversial is Woolf's suggestion that we look for signs
of sexual difference where we find them in life—not so much in
the rhythms or erotics of the text, but in its physiognomy. Woolf
speculated that a woman's style reflected the proportions and
nervous organization of her body, which was generally shorter,
more supple, and more compact than a man's. Hence her sentences would be shaped around a different center of gravity, as it
were. That a woman should write *as* a body—or let us say an
embodied being—and not as an angel of indeterminate or non-
existent sex seemed a more important point for Woolf to make
than to describe her literary anatomy. To surmount the habits of
mental chastity imposed by patriarchy and tell the truth about
the body were the special challenges facing women seriously committed to writing.

Yet Woolf, who virtually taught us how to understand and interpret sex-consciousness in literature, is equally adamant in pre-

scribing its sublimation into more impersonal modes of consciousness. For one thing, and it is the *primary* thing, heightened sex-consciousness limits our imaginative capacity and thus distorts our view of reality:

> To cast out and incorporate in a person of the opposite sex all that we miss in ourselves and desire in the universe and detest in humanity is a deep and universal instinct on the part both of men and women. But though it affords relief, it does not lead to understanding. Rochester is as great a travesty of the truth about men as Cordelia is of the truth about women.[56]

Not surprisingly, it was Coleridge, the pure critic, who guides Woolf to the "soul" of the problem with his claim that a great mind is androgynous. Woolf hazards that Coleridge meant by this that the "androgynous mind is resonant and porous; that it transmits emotion without impediment; that it is naturally creative, incandescent and undivided."[57] To confirm this theory, Woolf turns to the exemplary artist who never lost his composure before reality—Shakespeare. She repeatedly characterizes Shakespeare as a writer whose mind had consumed all impediments and impurities so that it would be impossible to say what he personally thought of women or what causes he held most dear. The ordinary mind is riven by severances and oppositions, swayed by loves and aversions, but the creative mind, the Shakespearean mind, consummates these opposites, mates what is female to what is male in human consciousness, expresses itself in perfect fullness, peace, and freedom.

All this, of course, is a myth, as Woolf well knew. But to characterize her account of the Shakespearean mind as a myth is not to say her account represents a fantasy. On the contrary, Shakespeare stands for the writer who lives at enmity with unreality; he has fought the battles of the world and won. Shakespeare abides in Woolf's critical imagination as a continuous presence whose spirit animates every writer who fixes her vision on reality, determined not to let it escape, or disappear, without a trace. Woolf concludes all her great tracts of the 1930s, when the fate of reading and writing seemed darkest, with an appeal to common fellowship between reader and writer, both of whom share common responsibility in preserving and creating reality. Thus if it is absolutely indispensable to write, and preferable to read, in a room of one's own, it is equally advisable that the windows not be shuttered, so that the outlines of "things as they are" can be kept in plain sight.

In such moments of vision we will find, Woolf assures us, the thing that endures change, survives catastrophe: there we will come into contact with the "common life which is the real life and not the . . . little separate lives which we live as individuals."[58] There congregate Anon and the common reader, Shakespeare and his sister, Mary Beton and Mrs. Brown, all busily conversing in the mind of those common and astute readers who pick up a book and, taking one last glance out the window, resume their reading.

6

The World Writer

In the second chapter of *Orlando*, Woolf's transhistorical hero, despondent over his disgrace at Court and the flight of Sasha, the Russian princess who has bewitched him, retires to his great country house to nurse his wounds in solitude. There he succumbs to that besetting vice of the Elizabethan nobleman— writing. His biographer discloses that Orlando has long been "afflicted with a love of literature," the "fatal nature" of which is "to substitute a phantom for a reality" (O, 57) Seeking to relieve his disordered mind by populating it with phantoms of his own creation, he retrieves from the huge cabinet that houses his works one thick manuscript and one thin one. The long work, which he will never finish, is called "Xenophila, a Tragedy." The thin one, which he will complete and publish centuries later, is entitled "The Oak Tree."

The literary joke is, of course, jingoistic. "Xenophila" reeks, in its multisyllabic ostentation and, indeed, its etymological inspiration, of the foreign. The name seems chosen to parody the ornate diction of high Elizabethan culture (the "contorted cogitations" and "delicate articulation" of Sir Thomas Browne's *Hydriotaphia. Urne-Burlai* is a great favorite and model for the aspiring writer). To the robust Anglo-Saxon temperament, "The Oak Tree," the only monosyllabic title in the stash of Orlando's unfinished work, clearly recommends itself for its terse and vigorous English, rooted in native idiom as well as native soil. "Xenophila" can claim no such authentic or sturdy provenance. The Greeks had no such word, being generally inhospitable to what was *xenos*—odd, unusual, hence foreign—a fact and attitude indicated by the word they did donate to us, *barbarian*, which initially referred to the non-Greek world and their offending, primitive speech. They did, however, entertain Xenophilos[1] as a masculine name. Perhaps, then, Woolf's feminized transliteration is a sly verbal portent of the sex change Orlando himself will later undergo. Perhaps, too, Orlando hoped that his tragedy would eventually convert the (invented) proper name, Xenophila, into a radiant substantive noun, *xenophilia*, a love of the foreign.

Still, whatever Orlando (or Woolf) intended by this title, the fact remains that, narratively, the tragic story of Xenophila or of the *xenophilia* she might have promoted in the world remained unfinished by Orlando and unknown to us. Is it foolish to wonder why? Xenophila's suspect provenance shouldn't have deterred Orlando from seeking solace in this new word and the work it inspired, for surely an Elizabethan poet would not shy at neologism. Perhaps Orlando lost interest or confidence in the work, as he might have in the word, because he wrongly conceived of *xenophi-*

lia as a subject for tragedy. Perhaps an embodied love of the foreign is more fittingly the material of comedy, a genre that generally entertains happier fates for those enchanted by brave new worlds and their wondrous people.

Certainly the comic note is more characteristic of Woolf's attitude whenever she encounters strangeness, whether in herself or in others. Unlike many other modernists of her generation, she was not especially well traveled, nor did her artistic identity depend on the soul-dislocating experience of exile to bring it to independent maturity. *Xenophilia* does not entail for her any physical or moral act of expatriation, but a more homely, if I may risk the pun, relation to the non-British world. Her voyages out were primarily imaginative ones, and while that made her more stay-at-home than Conrad or Joyce, she became as much an international modernist as they. Moreover, she identified with whoever and whatever was considered eccentric and outlandish in her own culture: she in fact prided herself in being an outsider excluded from the ranks of such proper British institutions as the army, the judiciary, the church, even the university, all of whose insider customs—and costumes— she satirizes in *A Room of One's Own* and *Three Guineas*. Her fiction also betrays an inordinate fondness for those characters who flout decorum, perhaps nowhere more superbly than in her indulgent portraits of the reckless Sally Seton, with her power to shock and to make Clarissa Dalloway "feel, for the first time, how sheltered the life at Bourton was" (MD, 36); and of the interloper Mrs. Manresa, who breaks the ice in the emotionally chilled atmosphere of Pointz Hall with the impulsive vibrations of her own "wild heart." Still, however fervently I might catalog and celebrate the non-British improprieties she champions in her fiction, many might hesitate to proclaim Woolf a world writer.

It is a hesitation that must be acknowledged by anyone seriously contemplating Woolf as a writer across cultures. Admittedly, I find the mere thought of Woolf extending her imaginative reach and influence across cultures a heartening and stimulating one. But however happy and productive, it is a thought that is shadowed by the remembrance that Virginia Woolf entered the ranks of world literature wearing the mantle of a London provincial— the lady-novelist from Bloomsbury. This image persists, despite recent scholarship exploring her imaginative and public involvement with the global politics of imperialism, of race, and of totalitarian wars.[2] There is something centripetal as well as centrifugal about Woolf's writing and social imagination that persistently pulls her into the gravitational field of Englishness and all that Englishness entails—its manners, traditions, values, and humors.

The assessments offered on the occasion of her death, though laudatory and, under the circumstances, respectful of her achievement, tended to confine her to this restricted cultural domain. Stephen Spender, an admiring friend, concludes that "the artistic aims in Virginia Woolf's novels are far more varied than the material, which is somewhat narrow and limited."[3] Limitation is also diplomatically suggested in Malcolm Cowley's review of the posthumous *Between the Acts*, in which he pronounced that "The spirit if not the body of Georgian England survives in her novels."[4] Cowley's is not an untrue nor even unkind pronouncement, although much more is recorded and preserved in that novel, and indeed in all of Woolf's work, however local her settings might be, than the spirit of Georgian England.

This Erich Auerbach understood when, from the lofty and lonely vantage point of scholarly exile, he surveyed the expanse of Western literature from the Hebrews and Greeks to the modern day and awarded Woolf a primary place among modernists who inherited and transformed the Western traditions of mimesis. Auerbach was the first critic of comparative instincts to understand the profound and unifying multiculturalism (although this would not be his word, but ours) heralded in Woolf's revolutionary realism. He recognized her audacity in seeking reality in the fidgeting of a restless little boy obliged to hold still as his mother took the measure for a brown stocking, and in the thoughts that such a commonplace sight might provoke in a group of vacationers, some of whom have philosophical training and so might ponder the symbolic and human import of such a domestic scene, but most of whom do not and so respond to this moment and its beauty in an undisciplined but emotionally significant way. As Auerbach almost triumphantly notes in closing his magisterial work, Woolf's novelistic materials might seem somewhat narrow and limited, but that did not prevent her from seeing in and through them "the determining factors in our real lives." In her exploration of the apparently random moment, Auerbach concludes, "something new and elemental appeared: nothing less than the wealth of reality and depth of life in every moment to which we surrender ourselves without prejudice."[5]

To surrender without prejudice—this, I would propose, is the moral imperative and defining act of a world writer. To respond to experience unaccompanied by native and personal bias is to enter into life unaided, but also unhindered, by the customs and conventions of inculcated ways of thought. In the modernists' unprejudiced surrender to the moment that absorbed them, Auerbach foresaw the triumph of a noncoercive universalism based on the rudimentary and common experiences of everyday life. Auerbach movingly describes the logic of this paradox:

It is precisely the random moment which is comparatively independent of the controversial and unstable orders over which men fight and despair; it passes unaffected by them, as daily life. The more it is exploited, the more the elementary things which our lives have in common come to light. The more numerous, varied, and simple the people are who appear as subjects of such random moments, the more effectively must what they have in common shine forth.[6]

To surrender without prejudice is thus to release that part of the mind unconscious or unregarding of tribal, communal, or national divisions and beliefs so that it may experience the moment before it has entered history, encounter reality before it has been seized and distorted by ideology. The fruit of this surrender, as Auerbach's language suggests, is the modern epiphany, in which the common life shines forth.

I do not believe Auerbach's choice of Woolf to exemplify this new world writing was an arbitrary one. But her exemplary achievement in excavating the common ground between and across cultures has largely been obscured by the Bloomsburyean garb that has frequently camouflaged as much as it has adorned her figure as an author. To appreciate how Woolf achieved her own unprejudiced surrender to the moment and to the common life it bodies forth, I would like to divest her of these garments and to displace, if not completely uproot, her from her native ground. So imagined, Woolf appears to me as a writer whose claim to world eminence is justified by her quite personal understanding and incorporation of non-British traditions, traditions that shaped her, as much if not more than did Bloomsbury, as a distinctly modern writer. I want to isolate the two traditions that she continually revisited, as if returning to a second imaginative home: Russian literature and Greek culture, especially its drama.

Both were traditions that attracted her in large part because—in social mores, emotional habits, and language—they were so utterly different from her own. Their very apartness suggested to her a world richer in realities than were ever dreamed of in Bloomsbury. She returned again and again to Greek and Russian literature for stimulus, sometimes for comfort, but always to behold and confront a reality or spiritual truth not readily discernible by English moral habits of thought. In Greek literature she found "the stable, the permanent, the original human being";[7] in Russian literature she was awed by "the soul that is the chief character in Russian fiction," the soul that "is not restrained by barriers," no matter how well-fortified, and so "overflows . . . floods . . . mingles with the souls of others."[8] Through her reading of the Greeks, whom she famously admitted she had no hope of really knowing, and the Russians, whose point of view she recognized as a major influence on European modernists, Woolf reached back into time and across the European continent to produce her most modern and urgent work. Such imaginative breadth, encompassing cultures remote in time or distanced by space and ideology, qualifies her as a world writer and helps us understand the very criteria by which a world writer might be identified and measured: historical depth as well as geographical reach; the imaginative capture within and across cultures of the random moment in which the elementary, thus shared, basis of existence manifests itself.

But this is putting the case abstractly, a mode Woolf always suspected. As both novelist and critic, she always subjected working theories and their underlying assumptions to the test of concrete experience. Let me then turn to her own account of an exemplary and characteristically droll instance of such imaginative participation in a life at once foreign and startlingly familiar to her. It is reported in a review of Chekhov's *The Cherry Orchard*. Recalling the delights of a 1920 production of the Arts Theatre at St. Martin's Theatre, Woolf reflects that there is nothing in English literature in the least like Chekhov's play. "It may be," she speculates,

> that we are more advanced, less advanced, or have advanced in an entirely different direction. At any rate, the English person who finds himself at dawn in the nursery of Madame Ranevskaia feels out of place, like a foreigner brought up with entirely different traditions. But these traditions are not (this, of course, is a transcript of individual experience) so ingrained in one as to prevent one from shedding them not only without pain but with actual relief and abandonment.[9]

Woolf's xenophilia here takes an active emotional form. Her imaginative readiness to shed preconceptions quickly intensifies into positive relief, indeed outright emotional abandon. It is as if her mind at such moments is suddenly freed from the force of cultural gravity that has kept it pinioned to its native ground and is spirited way into a radically unfamiliar way of experiencing and feeling life.

This seems almost literally to be the case when Woolf proceeds to describe her reactions to the performance. She reports the sensation of being transported to an imaginative horizon where "we have reached the end of everything: where space seems illimitable and time everlasting." In this sublime and completely imaginary space, she tries, "quite wrongly" she concedes, "to give effect to my sense that the human soul is free from all trappings and crossed incessantly by thoughts and emotions which wing their way from here, from there, from the furthest horizons—."[10] Surrender without prejudice can take no more extreme form than such cross-cultural exhilaration, a deep breathing, as it were, in which all the noxious fumes of chauvinism are exhaled. I deliberately make my own critical metaphors extravagant because Woolf encourages us, I think, not to shy away from irreverent, even outlandish, retorts to home culture. Examples are legion, but perhaps none more appropriate than her sly parody of Orlando's nativist credulity in believing the tales brought back by imperial adventurers that "the women in Muscovy wear beards and the men are covered in fur from the waist down; that both sexes are smeared with tallow to keep the cold out, tear meat with their fingers and live in huts where an English lord would scruple to keep his cattle" (O, 35–36). Hirsute, insulated by greasy tallow, brutish in table manners and habitation—it is easy to ridicule such caricatures and a relief to be rid of the ignorance, bolstered by self-approving complacency, that conspire in their creation.

Woolf Across Cultures

And yet Woolf would not be the world writer she is if she did not admit to the more intransigent habits of thought and feeling that can impede our imaginative surrender and allow the random moment to pass before it has yielded the wealth of life it shelters. Before venturing across cultures, Woolf always pauses to assess not so much the risks but the inevitable disappointments and failures that await her—or anyone—imaginatively drawn to whatever is foreign to them. Her attempt to describe the "Russian Point of View" in an essay of that name thus opens with this warning: "A special acuteness and detachment, a sharp angle of vision the foreigner will often achieve; but not that absence of self-consciousness, that ease and fellowship and sense of common values which make for intimacy and sanity and the quick give and take of familiar intercourse."[11] Woolf never attempts, much less accomplishes, her own acts of translation without acknowledging this moment of awkward unease when the mind in its transit suddenly, if not unexpectedly, finds itself in the presence of the utterly different.

Initially, however, Woolf treats the cross-cultural encounter as an occasion for reflection and, quite often, untroubled amusement. One such occasion of irrespressible British humor excited her comment in her review of *The Cherry Orchard*:

It occurred in the middle of Charlotte's strange speech in the beginning of the second act. "I have no proper passport. I don't know how old I am; I always feel I am still young," she begins. She goes on, "When I grew up I became a governess. But where I came from and who I am, I haven't a notion. Who my parents were—*very likely they weren't married*—I don't know." At the words I have italicised, Dunyasha bounced away from her to the other end of the bench, with an arch humour which drew the laugh it deserved. Miss Helena Millais seemed to be delighted to have this chance of assuring us that she did not believe a word of this morbid nonsense, and that the old jokes still held good in the world of sanity round the corner. But it was Miss Ethel Irving who showed the steadiest sense of what decency requires of a British matron in extremity. How she did it, since she spoke her part accurately, it is difficult to say, but her mere presence upon the stage was enough to suggest that all the comforts and all the decencies of English upper-class life were at hand, so that any moment her vigil upon the bench might have been appropriately interrupted by a manservant bearing a silver tray. "The Bishop is in the drawing-room, m'lady." "Thank you, Parker. Tell his Lordship I will come at once."[12]

On the outskirts of Chekhov's histrionic world of emotional extremity is the British world of sanity where all spiritual perplexities can be dismissed as morbid nonsense. As a playgoer, Woolf might have shared in the laughter, but as a world writer, she is ready to defect from the known world of custom and decency in which sanity decorously presides and imaginatively surrender to the emotionally foreign, extravagant, somewhat ridiculous behavior of people so unlike herself.

Still, lurking in this jovial anecdote of an evening spent in the company of Chekhov's characters is a less happy realization. In the moment of cross-cultural identification, Woolf is less hopeful than Auerbach that the unification of cultures and peoples is at hand. Auerbach explored the aesthetic paradox that in surrender there is victory—and to the victor goes the wealth of life. But readers willing to follow Woolf across cultures find a different, less sanguine paradox awaiting them: it is precisely in the realm of commonly held values, which makes possible the intimacy, sanity, and give-and-take of familiar intercourse in any given culture, that the search for common ground often proves most futile. Only a new understanding of what the common might encompass can resolve the paradox that Woolf's writings pose for us.

We can see Woolf struggling to come to terms with this paradox in her great essay "On Not Knowing Greek." The ignorance freely proclaimed in the essay's famous title concerns not only "difference of race and tongue but a tremendous breach of tradition."[13] Nowhere is this breach more dramatically evident than in our attempts to comprehend the language and agitated emotions of the Greek choruses. What we might call the Woolfian paradox of commonality asserts its objectionable presence at the very moment when, having shed our traditions, we are ready to hear the Greek tragic chorus voice the common values and shared feelings of their community. Yet instead of discovering what we have in common across cultures, we find ourselves stranded on the brink of utter incomprehension. As Woolf describes it:

> One must be able to pass easily into those ecstasies, those wild and apparently irrelevant utterances, those sometimes obvious and commonplace statements, to decide their relevance or irrelevance, to give them their relation to the play as a whole.
>
> We must "be able to pass easily"; but that of course is exactly what we cannot do. For the most part the choruses, with their obscurities, must be spelt out and their symmetry mauled.[14]

We must "be able to pass easily"; but that of course is exactly what we cannot do. Woolf quotes, then corrects herself at the very point that, assuming the convivial we, she genially purports to speak for us. But she is also now speaking *to* us as a writer who knows how

difficult such acts of translation are and who warns us that "to pass
easily" into the feelings and thoughts of a foreign culture is, as she
says "exactly what we cannot do." The adverb "exactly" functions
as an emotional as well as linguistic bar to our presumption that
the passage across time and cultures is so easily accomplished.[15]

Woolf across cultures is thus a figure precariously straddled
across a gap, wide and perhaps unbridgeable, that separates here
from there, the known from the unfamiliar world, the native from
the foreign, our words for things and for relations from theirs.
Being a writer, Woolf hesitates most anxiously on the threshold
of language itself, where cultures are most articulate—and most
stubbornly themselves. The world writer who seeks the common
life uniting people across cultures finds that words themselves re-
fuse to act as transparent and efficient vehicles of common feeling.
Woolf typically notices these obdurate opacities in meaning, not
in the refined and abstruse vocabulary of elites, but in the ordinary
words of everyday life. Let me cite an instance she frequently in-
vokes to illustrate this vernacular divide. In trying to isolate what
is unique and virtually untranslatable in the Russian lexicon of
feeling, Woolf remarks that the English

> cannot say "Brother" with simple conviction. . . . The En-
> glish equivalent for "Brother" is "Mate"—a very different
> word, with something sardonic in it, an indefinable sugges-
> tion of humour. Met though they are in the depths of mis-
> fortune the two Englishmen who thus accost each other will,
> we are sure, find a job, make their fortunes, spend the last
> years of their lives in luxury, and leave a sum of money to
> prevent poor devils from calling each other "Brother" on
> the Embankment. But it is common suffering, rather than

common happiness, effort or desire that produces the sense of brotherhood.[16]

In an earlier version of this essay, she had explained more fully this difference in emotional address:

> The truth is that if you say 'brother' you must say it with conviction, and it is not easy to say it with conviction. The Russians themselves produce this sense of conviction not because they acquiesce or tolerate indiscriminately or despair, but because they believe so passionately in the existence of the soul. . . . And that alone is important; that living core which suffers and toils is what we all have in common. We tend to disguise or to decorate it; but the Russians believe in it, seek it out, interpret it, and, following its agonies and intricacies, have produced not only the most spiritual of modern books but also the most profound.[17]

Here what I have called the Woolfian paradox of commonality, a paradox first perceived by Woolf in the context of world literature and culture, takes a curious turn, one that explains her debt to the Russian point of view for sharpening her own modernist vision. According to Woolf, the Russians have a language, fully expressive of their spiritual outlook, that puts them in direct contact with the living core in which, she believes, all cultural differences are dissolved. They make no effort to clothe the soul in proper garments or festoon it with ceremonial dress. Nothing distracts them from seeing this living core as the fundamental and complex reality of human existence. As a proper Englishwoman, Woolf can only observe and try to describe the rich language and profound works in which this reality is netted and made manifest. She can never approach the soul in the same words, follow it into the deepest recesses of life, as the Russians so intrepidly yet so "naturally" do.

Still, there are moments when Woolf nevertheless experiences a sensation beyond the capacity of her native culture to produce and her native language to articulate. Such a moment is remembered at the conclusion of her review of that memorable performance of *The Cherry Orchard*: "I do not know how better to describe the sensation at the end of *The Cherry Orchard*, than by saying that it sends one into the street feeling like a piano played upon at last, not in the middle only but all over the keyboard and with the lid left open so that sound goes on."[18] Like a piano played upon at last, Woolf experiences, through Chekhov's great, indisputably *Russian* play, the full sounding of her nature. In this moment of bodily as well as emotional "transport," she is translated into a realm outside language, indeed almost beyond culture, yet finds herself at home in the world in a new way.

Ideological and cultural critics might admonish us about the dangers, not to mention hauteur, of this kind of mutual identification not only across cultures but across historical eras. Woolf's achievement stubbornly defies such reproaches. Certainly Auerbach saw in modernism's embrace of the random moment the chance not only to render "in a very personal way the individual who lives in it," but "also (and for that very reason) . . . the elementary things which men in general have in common."[19] Readers of Woolf will appreciate how the word common resonates here in a profound way, given the distinctive place that word occupies in her fictional and critical view of the world. What is most valued and yet necessarily most elusive and fugitive in her moral imaginings is our common nature, whether that nature is embodied in the common reader to whom she entrusted, following the precedent established by Dr. Johnson, the task of deciding all claims to literary honors, or manifested in the subject to which she continually returns in her novels—"the common life which is the real life." This is the common life and common interest that she tirelessly advances in her polemical writings, most ardently at the conclusion of *Three Guineas*: "A common interest unites us; it is one world, one life."[20]

Woolf, then, was not afraid to trust, indeed to venture all her moral credibility on that democratically humble but morally resonant, imposingly grave word. In enlisting the "common" as her most trusted moral ally and artistic arbiter, she was not flirting with essentialism, nor was she indulging an imperialist fantasy of similitude. It was a word whose origin, history, and, if you pardon the redundancy, common usage sanctified her vision of one world, one life. We should also note that this modest word has its origin in the Latin *communis*, indicating what is shared by all or by many and which carries within it a history of mutual obligations (*com*, with, plus *munus*, services rendered). The word "common" thus emerges out of a communal practice of social and moral barter, a mutual and mutually beneficial exchange of duties, rights, and values that bind communities. These communal bonds, in turn, effectively work to affirm and indeed help create a world order that supersedes as it transcends national or local boundaries.

One ironic consequence of the paradox of commonality is that at times only a foreign language, as Woolf repeatedly reminds us, can convey an attitude or feeling that we experience but cannot name. Thus she notes how the Greeks fashioned words "which, in so many instances, we have made expressive to us of our own emotions, Θάλασσα, Θάνατος, ἄάθος, ἄστήρ, σελήνη—to take the first that come to hand; so clear, so hard, so intense, that to speak plainly yet fittingly without blurring the outline or clouding the depths Greek is the only expression."[21] The sea, death, flower, star, moon: as she enumerates these clear, hard words for emotions that baffle the expressive power of English, Woolf appears to us as a kind of castaway, thrown up on an unknown shore, picking through shards of a poetic tradition that emit their siren call to her.

But at other times Woolf is lured by those flashes of poetry that leave us "without the support of words," contemplating a "meaning . . . just on the far side of language": "It is the meaning which in moments of astonishing excitement and stress we perceive in our minds without words; it is the meaning that Dostoevsky (hampered as he was by prose and as we are by translation) leads us to by some astonishing run up the scale of emotions and points at but cannot indicate; the meaning that Shakespeare succeeds in snaring."[22] Arguably, then, it is on the far side of language where world literature abides, awaiting its readers and common, that is, its best, interpreters. It is on the far side of language that the genius of Sophoclean drama, Dostoevsky's soul-epics, and Shakespeare's theater are copresent. There, too, is where we might get fitful intimations of something that is not only beyond our local culture but beyond our native stock of words. There we will find "not the thing itself, but the reverberations and reflection which, taken into [the] mind, the thing has made, close enough to the original to illustrate it, remote enough to heighten, enlarge, and make splendid."[23]

Of course it is one thing to undertake such expansive flights beyond the range of clear meanings, and another to bring oneself back to earth. To this glimpse of a heightened, enlarged, and splendid universe beyond language, perhaps indeed beyond the human capacity for sustained experience, Woolf could only oppose the inclination of her own mind, with its bias for hearty, sensible British "humour." It was humor that Woolf relied on to dissolve what was foreign to her language and experience—the strophes and antistrophes of the Greek chorus, the Russian fraternal hail of Brother—and reconstitute them in the idiom and manners of her native English.

Thus even as she celebrates the Russian's spiritual profundity, she suddenly sees, in a spasm of nativist humor, the virtues of a countervoice, "the voice of protest . . . the voice of another and an ancient civilisation which seems to have bred in us the instinct to enjoy and fight rather than to suffer and understand. English fiction from Sterne to Meredith bears witness to our natural delight in humour and comedy, in the beauty of earth, in the activities of the intellect, and in the splendour of the body."[24] Her English delight in humor and comedy is also thwarted in her encounter with the Greeks. Tellingly, one of the lamentable consequences of not knowing Greek is not knowing when to laugh in reading Greek:

> To laugh instantly it is almost necessary (though Aristophanes may supply us with an exception) to laugh in English. Humour, after all, is closely bound up with a sense of the body. When we laugh at the humour of Wycherley, we are laughing with the body of that burly rustic who was our common ancestor on the village green. The French, the Italians, the Americans, who derive physically from so different a stock, pause, as we pause in reading Homer, to make sure

that they are laughing in the right place, and the pause is fatal. Thus humour is the first of the gifts to perish in a foreign tongue, and when we turn from Greek to English literature it seems, after a long silence, as if a great age were ushered in by a burst of laughter.[25]

Rather than being pained by "the doubts and difficulties" that prevent us from laughing where and how the Greeks would laugh, Woolf delights in an English guffaw that is as hearty as it is welcome. English humor allows Woolf to indulge her chauvinism without apology, indeed with something like patriotic relish.

I think we should take this burst of laughter as a healthy sign. We know from Freud that humor functions as a mode of self-defense for the threatened ego, which refuses, he writes, "to be distressed by the provocations of reality, to let itself be compelled to suffer. It insists that it cannot be affected by the traumas of the external world; it shows, in fact, that such traumas are no more than occasions for it to gain pleasure."[26] He went on to speculate that humor has its origin in the benign parental agency, which, internalized in the super-ego, "speaks kindly words of comfort to the intimidated ego."[27] Doesn't humor also incorporate the benign influence of the parental culture, which exerts a salutary centripetal pressure on the centrifugal xenophilic imagination? Humor, we thus might speculate, prevented Woolf from being drawn irresistibly and helplessly into the orbit of the Russians, with their soulfulness and sadness, or of the Greeks, who, "[w]ith the sound of the sea in their ears, vines, meadows, rivulets about them, . . . are even more aware than we are of a ruthless fate."[28] These were two cultures that in Woolf's estimation had penetrated to the very core of life and reported what they saw there without mitigation. But as Freud reminds us, "Humour is not resigned; it is rebellious. It signifies not only the triumph of the ego but also of the pleasure principle, which is able here to assert itself against the unkindness of the real circumstances."[29] Given her own temperamental disposition to melancholia, Woolf was a writer who in her representations of reality knew how to minister to herself. Rebellious, pleasure-seeking, self-delighting British humor allows Woolf to assimilate what she encounters in other cultures into her own language and writing without being over-whelmed or herself denatured.

So let us return for a last time to our guiding image of Woolf straddled across cultures, suspended between the recognition that we are the same and the knowledge that we are different. This double relation is figured in a brief exchange in *Between the Acts* between Lucy Swithin, the unifier caressing her cross, and the lyric poet Isa, who seeks unity in other spiritual registers. It occurs at the conclusion of the pageant:

> "Did you feel," [Lucy] asked, "what he said: we act different parts but are the same?"
> "Yes," Isa answered. "No," she added. It was Yes, No. Yes, yes, yes the tide rushing out embracing. No, no. no, it con-tracted. The old boot appeared on the shingle. (BA, 215)

This dynamic counterpoint between yes and no, affirmation and remonstration, constitutes the double rhythm that the world writer translates into his or her own national idiom. Isa's "yes" betokens the relief, then active abandon, of the mind as it rushes to embrace the foreign, the strange, the excitingly different, in hopes of finding in that embrace an elemental nature, the utterly common. The "no" that inevitably follows betokens the necessary countermovement of the mind withdrawing into its own native, often isolated dwelling. Was there ever an image of defiance and negation, more droll, almost pitifully so, than that old boot on the shingle? Yet it is the humor in that image of a homely, dilapidated, but comfortable old boot marooned atop the surviving homestead that makes, Woolf seems to imply, our human and cultural separateness bearable.[30]

Woolf's complex understanding of how cultures interact with and influence one another prompts me to propose her as the personification of her own neologism. She heralds the arrival of the new Xenophila, the modern writer who loves the foreign both for its own and for our common sake. When I asked a friend of mine who teaches classical literature about this arresting word, he remarked that as a neologism it indeed might be pronounced to sound like a proper name. And then he added, "Something that might interest you is a late commentator of Euripides. In the *Life of Euripides* attested in the scholia to his extant plays, Euripides is said to have been 'xenophilotatos' (adj. in superlative), because he was much loved by foreigners. [As you can see, in this late attestation the term has passive sense.] Loving foreigners was foreign to our dear ancient Greeks! But nothing could prevent them from being loved by foreigners."[31] In this particular respect, then, Woolf was superior to her dear Greeks, or at least was most like her beloved Antigone, whose self-declared nature was to join in loving. This would be the image of Woolf I would urge her readers to entertain—not Woolf the English lady of letters, but the cosmopolitan Xenophila Xenophilotatos, the world writer, who, as her writings and her readership attest, loved and was much loved by foreigners across cultures.

7

The Adventurer

WOOLF'S SENSE OF ADVENTURE

Even those willing to greet Woolf as a world writer might balk at
hailing her as an adventurer. This reluctance is understandable, as
long as the sense of adventure is a commonly held and traditional
one.[1] But in or about December 1910, the sense of adventure seems
to have changed. Woolf noted the change and helped provoke as
well as prepare for it. Retrospectively she greeted it when, in *A
Room of One's Own*, she turned her critical gaze from the epic age
of women's writing to the literature of her own time and selected,
apparently at random, a novel bearing the somewhat generic and
slightly breathless title, *Life's Adventure*.[2] That book, which dares
to proclaim that Chloe likes Olivia and in doing so to break the
sequence—of desire, of narrative—that the traditional novel re-
lentlessly, if imaginatively, pursued, inspired Woolf's deepest re-
flections on the relation of women, writing, and modernity.

In analyzing that new and not yet stable relation, Woolf notes, first of all, that *Life's Adventure* is representative of a recent outcrop of fiction written by women that treats subjects and dramatizes relationships that a generation ago very few, if any, women would have dared represent so openly. This unexpected boldness in subject matter is initially what distinguishes the contemporary from the epic age of women's writing, whose "natural simplicity"—a term of praise rather than condescension in Woolf's critical vocabulary—has yielded to a literature exhibiting "a wider range, a greater subtlety."[3] The wider range and greater subtlety of experience dramatized in works like *Life's Adventure* signal that women's writing no longer springs exclusively from an autobiographical urge. Woolf regards this development as a promising sign that women increasingly regard literature primarily as an art rather than as a form of self-expression.

Still, as Woolf quickly realized, the modern sense of adventure is only partly characterized by its bold subject matter or its unprecedented frankness in declaring that women like women, that many women have and enjoy a life and work outside the home, that love need not be the sole interpreter of women's existence. An adventure encompasses more than an experience marked by risk and brimming with possibilities of death or self-transfiguration. Adventure is not experienced or even recognizable *as* an adventure unless and until the mind acknowledges the possibilities of extinction or exaltation that the adventure fortuitously but fatefully presents. There is no adventure, but thinking makes it so. Put more dramatically, even pathologically, it is only the adventurer who makes for the heart of darkness because it *is* a heart of darkness.

Conrad's tales of adventure, notable for their subdued tone and ponderous narration, are disquieting glosses on this psychological fact. Their heavy air of moral subtlety emanates from Conrad's suspicion of the adventure, which attracts the foolhardy as well as the brave, the reckless as well as the idealistic, the Browns as well as the Lord Jims, the Kurtzes as well as the Marlows of the world. Conrad reserves his deepest moral admiration not for the adventurer, but for the reliable man of steady habit and fixed purpose. However heroic their conduct may appear, and in fact may actually be, his most trusted mariners and sea captains are those most disposed to do their duty rather than to question it. Their function in Conrad's fiction is to serve as the custodians of our settled conceptions of light and order, that is, to uphold the code of the anti-adventurer. The anti-adventurer, so employed, is not so much opposed to adventure as oblivious to it; his code of duty and ethics of work mentally insulate him from the awareness that he is within the vicinity, if not in the actual midst, of an adventure.

Women have been traditionally debarred from adventure because their consciousness has been similarly insulated, not by temperament, but by social and narrative custom whose regulatory law is epitomized in Roland Barthes's narrative axioms: "Woman is sedentary; Man hunts, journeys. Woman is faithful (she waits); Man is fickle (he sails away, he cruises)."[4] Heroines of the traditional novel rarely take to the open road or the high seas; they are characterized and venerated as indwelling spirits of the shore. Traditionally they have been assigned the task of creating and providing shelter—the shelter of a home, of a marriage, of a civilized enclave like the Ramsay household in *To the Lighthouse*, set on an island surrounded by choppy seas.

Women thus come rather late to the tradition of adventure in which life takes the form of an astonishing narrative. The summons to adventure accordingly issues from different sources in the world and from within the self, not just because they are women, but also because they are moderns, for whom there are fewer dark places of the earth, if more and more dark places of the mind, will, and spirit to explore. Mary Carmichael's *Life's Adventure*, Woolf proposes, exemplifies this new sense of adventure and the new female writing that it inspires, writing that is so untethered to the docks of traditional femininity that it induces in her a kind of readerly vertigo. Carmichael's writing, she reports,

> was like being out at sea in an open boat. Up one went, down one sank. This terseness, this short-windedness, might mean that she was afraid of something; afraid of being called "sentimental" perhaps; or she remembers that women's writing has been called flowery and so provides a superfluity of thorns; but until I have read a scene with some care, I cannot be sure whether she is being herself or some one else.[5]

What Woolf finds curious about this expedition into unknown representational waters is that as a writer, Mary Carmichael seems motivated by fear rather than by an eagerness to enjoy or to report new experiences. Moreover, Woolf suspects that the pace and rhythm of her narrative do not derive from the unconscious or instinctive motions of Carmichael's own mind, which, Woolf seems to suggest, feels a more natural affinity to the calmer and more uterine waters of the sentimental mode and so redoubles the effort to resist them. Mary Carmichael's terseness, being self-conscious, differs from the laconic manner of those absorbed in the immediate and dangerous business of navigating uncharted and often turbulent seas. Her thorny manner is not due to her impatience with obstructing convention. Rather it is defensive; she is trying to ward off the flowery, effeminate style associated with women taking their ease in sheltered, sunny gardens where rough winds hardly every blow.

These observations on narrative style and authorial attitude are not unconnected to the book's title and to the expectations aroused by its declaration that life is an adventure. Yet how are we to read that declaration? Is there something deliberately, even mischievously formulaic and possibly banal that the title is trying at once to evoke and denigrate? Is Woolf's psychologizing of adventure a feminist attempt to undermine masculinist bravado and the cult of daring physical exploration? Or is she genuinely attracted to the rough seas and extravagant motions of adventure that can carry her beyond the limits of her own experience into unbounded, possibly dangerous, realms of thought and feeling? *Life's Adventure* prompts me to wonder what adventure itself might mean to a novelist whose first book announced her urge, never abandoned nor fully satisfied, to voyage out, to ally herself, as Lily Briscoe unaccountably does in a rather bizarre moment in *To the Lighthouse*, with the "sailors and adventurers" (TTL, 104) of the world in her own artistic exploration of modern life and form.

Let our own exploration begin by considering that bizarre moment in order to determine whether Woolf is being herself or someone else—let us say an armchair Conrad—in her feeling for adventure. Lily's sudden and curious identification with sailors and adventurers comes as a kind of comment on Mrs. Ramsay's triumphant presentation of the *Boeuf en Daube*, a culinary wonder that, within the lavish symbolic economy of the novel, is endowed with the ritual status of a ceremonial dish. Lily, observing that triumph and Mrs. Ramsay's obvious enjoyment of her power to create community that it symbolizes, suddenly finds herself overcome "by the emotion, the vibration, of love" (TTL, 103). The feeling is one Lily has rather primly resisted, but for sensible, not prudish, reasons. It is not and cannot be pleasant to be overcome by a love that has no place in it for oneself, except as an accidental witness or supernumerary celebrant. Lily's residual sense of resistance surfaces even as Eros pulls her into its pleasurable wake. Unfortunately, her rebellion initially takes the abject, negative form of self-dissatisfaction: "How inconspicuous she felt herself by Paul's side! He, glowing, burning; she, aloof, satirical; he bound for adventure; she, moored to the shore: he launched, incautious; she, solitary, left out—and, ready to implore a share, if it were disaster, in his disaster, she said shyly: 'When did Minta lose her brooch?'" (TTL, 103–4). Paul at once answers and dismisses her question with an "an odd chuckle . . . as if he had said, Throw yourself off the cliff if you like, I don't care" and then further sears her spirit by turning "on her cheek the heat of love, its horror, its cruelty, its unscrupulosity" (TTL, 104).

In the face of this rebuff, Lily must contain her urge "to protest violently and outrageously her desire to help him, envisaging how in the dawn on the beach she would be the one to pounce on the brooch half-hidden by some stone, and thus herself be included among the sailors and adventurers" (TTL, 104). Although Lily's silent outburst is comically muffled by her own instinct for self-mockery, its emotional force and urgency is undeniable. Desire is speaking here, rather loudly I would say, insisting on making itself heard to us, who are, after all, the only ones who can really benefit from what it has to say about human needs and feelings.

But it is important not to mistake the emotional meaning of Lily's desire and the outrageous, if silent, outburst it provokes. Her sudden impulse to hurl herself into a company and an enterprise far removed from her habitual self and inclinations is not a sign that she is ready for love, but rather, that she is ready for adventure. Lily may be one of the first modern heroines not to confuse or conflate the two, not to believe—or despair—that love is the supreme life adventure possible for women. She wants to leave behind the caution and detachment that moor her to the shore and launch headlong into an adventure that would take her not just beyond her customary self, but beyond self-satire, which patrols the shores of consciousness with its merciless searchlights, ferreting out and exposing the ridiculous dreams, the preposterous but not abandoned hope of joining up with the sailors and adventurers to pursue a life for which it would otherwise seem she is entirely unsuited.

Lily's desire to venture beyond the ordinary courses of her life and to defy the emotional boundaries she routinely respects in her dealings with other people is what qualifies her to be considered, if not unambiguously confirmed, as a type of "The Adventurer," as Georg Simmel describes him in his essay of that title. Simmel's characterization of the adventurer as a pronounced social type, a distinct category of person, is founded on a particular understanding of what constitutes an actual adventure. "The most general form of adventure," Simmel asserts,

> is its dropping out of the continuity of life. "Wholeness of life," after all, refers to the fact that a consistent process runs

through the individual components of life, however crassly and irreconcilably distinct they may be. What we call an adventure stands in contrast to that interlocking of life-links, to that feeling that those countercurrents, turnings, and knots still, after all, spin forth a continuous thread. An adventure is certainly a part of our existence, directly contiguous with other parts which precede and follow it; at the same time, however, in its deeper meaning, it occurs outside the usual continuity of this life. Nevertheless, it is distinct from all that is accidental and alien, merely touching life's outer shell. While it falls outside the context of life, it falls, with this same movement, as it were, back into that context again . . . ; it is a foreign body in our existence which is yet somehow connected with the center; the outside, if only by a long and unfamiliar detour, is formally an aspect of the inside.[6]

Simmel's account of the temporal and spatial character of adventure at first may hardly seem promising for understanding a writer who declared her determination to record the random and variegated impressions of an ordinary mind on an ordinary day, the unexceptional and unadventurous life encountered on any Monday or Tuesday; nor does it seem to illuminate the special character of a novelist dedicated to tracking the ramifying and interlocking threads that knit one thought, one consciousness, one life to another in a continuous strand. Yet as we all know and have experienced, the strand can unravel, the threads become frayed. Rather than lament this tear in the fabric of the everyday, Woolf seizes upon it, like Lily, for its promise of adventure, for an experience, as Simmel defines it, that eccentrically departs from the customary, concentric rounds of life yet at the same time and in the same spiritual movement is reprojected into the center of the ego where meaning secludes itself.

This sense of adventure as a double and intrinsically centripetal movement, a voyage out that is simultaneously a voyage into and within the self, informs Woolf's experiments in modern narrative. It is an understanding that announces itself as early and as personally as 1905 in a letter to Lady Robert Cecil, who has been traveling to Japan and the Middle East: "I have just written a very vivid account of the desert myself," Woolf tells her. Then she adds: "I should have felt more at my ease in Japan. You and Violet seem to have explored each other with entirely successful results. I wish you would now write an account of that journey for me; I don't so much care for Red Seas, and Rocky Mountains, but I love this Human Inside."[7] The novelist in embryo is making a request, not for scenic description, but for reports on what transpires in that uncharted or underreported territory—this Human Inside. For Woolf, this Human Inside is at once the sphere and destination of all genuine adventure.

This Human Inside

Perhaps the most exultant yet troubled representation of the voyage within this Human Inside is that well-known and much remarked moment in *To the Lighthouse* when Mrs. Ramsay retreats from the novelistic surface composed of those countercurrents, turnings, and knots of successiveness over which she ordinarily presides and shrinks into a "wedge-shaped core of darkness, something invisible to others" (TTL, 65). As much as this wedge-shaped core of darkness might call to mind the triangular purple shape that represents Mrs. Ramsay in the picture Lily is painting throughout the novel, it has little of the painterly about it. In the novelist's eye, Mrs. Ramsay is reduced and condensed into a self without color, features, or textured surface, a self whose spiritual density paradoxically renders it invisible and highly mobile. This self, having shed it attachments, is now free, as the narrative relates, for the strangest adventures:

> When life sank down for a moment, the range of experience seemed limitless. And to everybody there was always this sense of unlimited resources, she supposed; one after another, she, Lily, Augustus Carmichael, must feel, our apparitions, the things you know us by, are simply childish. Beneath it is all dark, it is all spreading, it is unfathomably deep; but now and again we rise to the surface and that is what you see us by. Her horizon seemed to her limitless. There were all the places she had not seen; the Indian plains; she felt herself pushing aside the thick leather curtain of a church in Rome. This core of darkness could go anywhere, for no one saw it. (TTL, 65)

Mrs. Ramsay appears to enter a self-induced trance in which the bonds of habit and of social custom that tie consciousness to the visible, sensate world, are suddenly loosened and unknotted, freeing her—her what, mind? Soul? Consciousness?—freeing *something* within her for the strangest adventures.

There is nothing strange, however, about the feeling that links adventure to dream and trance states, as Simmel observes:

The more "adventurous" an adventure, that is, the more fully it realizes its idea, the more "dreamlike" it becomes in our memory. It often moves so far away from the center of the ego and the course of life which the ego guides and organizes that we may think of it as something experienced by another person. How far outside that course it lies, how alien it has become to that course, is expressed precisely by the fact that we might well feel that we could appropriately assign to the adventure a subject other than the ego.[8]

Following Simmel, we might provisionally conclude that Mrs. Ramsay is indeed having an adventure; in fact, she may never have been so adventurous as when her busy, fussing, and fretful "novelistic" ego contracts into a compact, featureless core of being, capable of motion but not of expression. Yet even though she can now go anywhere, and I assume feel anything, Mrs. Ramsay oddly reverts to emotions more proper to the old novelistic ego rather than to the new adventurous one:

> They could not stop it, she thought, exulting. There was freedom, there was peace, there was, most welcome of all, a summoning together, a resting on a platform of stability. Not as oneself did one find rest ever, in her experience (she accomplished here something dexterous with her needles) but as a wedge of darkness. Losing personality, one lost the fret, the hurry, the stir; and there rose to her lips always some exclamation of triumph over life when things came together in this peace, this rest, this eternity. (TTL, 65–66)

Despite the favorable portents attending the start of Mrs. Ramsay's adventure, something goes terribly wrong before it can establish itself *as* an adventure. Although she can go anywhere, Mrs. Ramsay prefers to seek out and seek rest upon a platform of stability, a platform that shields her not just from the ravages of life, but from the uncertainties and vicissitudes of adventure itself. More welcome to Mrs. Ramsay than the freedom of adventure is the feeling of having triumphed over an enemy, whom she identifies as Life, but which Woolf suggests, through the Grimms' fairy tale of "The Fisherman and his Wife" that Mrs. Ramsay has just finished reading to her son, may be larger than Life, may be, in fact, the Will and Order of the World.

This sense of triumph over Life at once rewards and spoils Mrs. Ramsay's adventure. It is a triumph too mixed up with her feelings for her ordinary, continuous, and islanded life of Monday and Tuesday, too little involved with the excitement in navigating the borderless world contiguous to, but nevertheless decidedly beyond, daily life. Some inhibiting force is at work that diverts her adventuring spirit and misleads it into the realm of quietism. Consequently, her adventure as a wedge of darkness within this great Human Inside—at once an unbounded field and a bottomless receptacle of consciousness in which "it is all dark, it is all spreading, it is unfathomably deep"—fails to disclose what underlies the fret and stir, all the inexpressive and insubstantial apparitions we see one another by. Her victory even begins to appear pyrrhic when its human meaning is belied rather than consecrated by the benediction she pronounces over it: "We are in the hands of the Lord." To her credit, Mrs. Ramsay recognizes that her words are insincere. She is annoyed by her own reassuring words, then disavows them as she returns to "her mind and to her heart, purifying out of existence that lie, any lie" (TTL, 66). However laudable, this act of expiation only confirms the conventionality of her gesture since it is performed by her mind and heart—conspicuously conventional terms that revive her workaday "novelistic" ego. Moreover, that lie, however purified, casts some doubt on the triumph that prompted it.

I think we cannot be too appreciative or too suspicious of Mrs. Ramsay's triumphs. To succumb to the authority established by those triumphs is to risk losing our sense—eventually our own need—of adventure. Triumph is the word summarizing Mrs. Ramsay's relation to the world (just as "risk," as Eudora Welty noted, is "the novel's repeated word").[9] Triumph is a word that alerts us that Mrs. Ramsay regards life not as an adventure to be pursued, but as a battle to be waged—and a losing battle at that. "The Window," the initial panel of the novel that celebrates her power, is a record of her triumphs in orchestrating an engagement between Paul and Minta; in getting Mr. Bankes to feast at her table, despite his misgivings about whether the vegetables will be cooked properly; in commanding life to stand still so that she might make something permanent of it.

This sense of triumph, as the narrative defines it, is allied to the sense of adventure but is not identical to it. Both the triumph and an adventure disrupt, rise above, or go beyond the uneventful continuities of everyday life. But in her triumphal mood, Mrs. Ramsay would halt and seek rest precisely where the spirit of adventure would have us move on. Mrs. Ramsay's strange adventures are excursions of being that mimic adventure in departing from the fret, the hurry, and the stir of ordinary life, but these adventurous possibilities are aborted by her own instincts for stability. If she were to write—or inspire, as she in fact does here—a book concerned with *Life's Adventure*, it would be filled with sudden frights and creeping menaces, but no sustained passages in open waters. It is not so much the limitless spaces but the fluidity of adventure that prevents Mrs. Ramsay from venturing off dry land or departing from her platform of stability. The real adventurer would risk plunging, as Lily Briscoe does, into those dark waters of annihilation. A modern adventurer would also understand, as Lily does, that you can plunge into those dark waters without ever leaving the shore.

So it is to Lily that we must turn, as Woolf herself turns in the last panel of the novel, to seek out the meaning of "Life's adventure":

> What was it then? What did it mean? Could things thrust their hands up and grip one; could the blade cut; the fist grasp? Was there no safety? No learning by heart of the ways of the world? No guide, no shelter, but all was miracle, and leaping from the pinnacle of a tower into the air? Could it be, even for elderly people, that this was life?—startling, unexpected, unknown? (TTL, 183)

Nothing is more modern than Lily's apprehension, but also her hope, that every moment promises to deliver us to a life of perpetual adventure—that is, a life in which every moment would appear to us as startling, unexpected, unknown. Lily at this particular moment is at once abandoned to and transfigured by her own modernity: she is without the guide or shelter of an enduring and continuous tradition; she is exposed to the lacerations of immediate sensation; she is vulnerable to the tenacious grip the desired things of this world exert against the ordinary relaxations of time and habit.

The unknown is the primal lure to adventure, but who could survive a life of unrelenting adventure, in which every moment would startle and surprise, in which life would not unfold, but erupt in one unprecedented and unpredictable experience after another? No horror of the conventional adventure tale can equal the shocks and terrors that await explorers of the Human Inside: even Conrad cannot approach Woolf in communicating the sheer terror of an adventure that is torn so violently and apparently irreparably out of the continuities of life. Conrad's narratives, after all, ease us into the regions where adventures lurk. They begin in a preternatural calm, proceed carefully and gradually into the heart of darkness, maintain their sedative mood of trance even in the midst of horrors, remain spellbound to the end. Only Woolf dares plunge[10] into that Human Inside where every moment at once promises and threatens to be the final adventure, the adventure that would leave the mind forever disconnected from those continuities of life and feeling in which ordinary reality, indeed sanity itself, is embedded. For Woolf the threshold of adventure is always imminent. There is at the heart of any given moment, hence at the heart of time itself, the promise— which is also the threat—of adventure. Her fiction describes no known defense against the shock of such moments of visionary intensity and in fact might be described as a record of her recovery from them.

There is a touch of madness, of course, in adventure pursued so maniacally into the heart of the present moment, but there is also a high comedy in Lily's "pitch of imbecility" as she imagines herself leaping from a pinnacle into thin air, like a cartoon charac-

ter who races off a cliff and only falls once she looks down and—
here is the miracle—somehow scrambles to safety or survives her
fall. Lily has such a comic moment of recovery when she steers
her thoughts toward the shores of the ordinary: "Heaven be
praised, no one had heard her cry that ignominious cry, stop pain,
stop! She had not obviously taken leave of her senses. No one had
seen her step off her strip of board into the waters of annihilation.
She remained a skimpy old maid, holding a paint-brush" (TTL,
184). Woolf is so buoyed by her comic will to adventure that she
can mock her own startling image of defenselessness before the
heartlessness of the world. So what if Life affords no more safety
than that provided by a little strip of board afloat in a watery
abyss! Lily's adventure seems less unnerving when she realizes that
she has *had* an adventure, albeit a momentary one, and not a bout
of madness.

So it is that Lily settles into a meditative and sublime calm she
attributes to the dozing Mr. Carmichael, as she approaches the
end of her own adventures and the close of the novel:

> So coming back from a journey, or after an illness, before
> habits had spun themselves across the surface, one felt that
> same unreality, which was so startling; felt something
> emerge. Life was most vivid then. One could be at one's
> ease. Mercifully one need not say, very briskly, crossing the
> lawn to greet old Mrs. Beckwith, who would be coming out
> to find a corner to sit in, "Oh, good-morning, Mrs. Beck-
> with! What a lovely day! Are you going to be so bold as to
> sit in the sun? Jasper's hidden the chairs. Do let me find you
> one!" and all the rest of the usual chatter. One need not
> speak at all. One glided, one shook one's sails (there was a

good deal of movement in the bay, the boats were starting
off) between things, beyond things. Empty it was not, but
full to the brim. She seemed to be standing up to the lips
in some substance, to move and float and sink in it, yes, for
these waters were unfathomably deep.[11] Into them had
spilled so many lives. The Ramsays'; the children's; and all
sorts of waifs and strays of things besides. A washer-woman
with her basket; a rook; a red-hot poker; the purples and
grey-greens of flowers: some common feeling which held
the whole. (TTL, 195)

I hope that by now it will be clear that the common feeling
that holds and binds the whole is the feeling of adventure. It is
the feeling of adventure that confers a vivid distinctness upon the
individual people and objects of the world—the washerwoman
with her basket, the isolated rook, the red-hot poker—extracting
them from their place in the continuum of everyday life, rendering them strange, even alien. The vivid individual life or object is
sharply preserved even as it is returned to the matrix of existence
between and beyond things. Spurred on by this resurgent and
distinctly modern sense of adventure, Lily, no longer moored to
the shore, joins at last the company of the sailors and adventurers.
That hers is a true, if imaginary, adventure is confirmed by the
course she sails, the course of all truly modern adventures, the
course between and beyond the everyday things of the mind and
of the world.

Woolf is figuratively representing here what Simmel regards as
the most profound inner manifestation of adventure, in which it
is not a segment of experience but life as a whole that is perceived
as an adventure. For this, Simmel advises us, "one need neither

be an adventurer nor undergo many adventures."[12] Some like-minded perception seems to be indicated by the title of Woolf's representative, if imaginary, modern work, *Life's Adventure*, for which Simmel's essay might serve as a gloss, and in fact has done so in this chapter. One need not be a conventional adventurer, may indeed appear his most abject and comic antitype—a skimpy old maid holding a paintbrush—and yet still be, in however unassuming, even diffident a guise, what Simmel calls an "adventurer of the spirit." The philosopher is one such adventurer, the Woolfian artist another. Both are engaged in what Simmel calls "the hopeless, but not therefore meaningless, attempt to form into conceptual knowledge an attitude of the soul, its mood toward itself, the world, God."[13]

Still, it is clear from the fictions that follow *To the Lighthouse* that Woolf's sense of adventure was not limited to the spirit alone, and that the knowledge she hoped to derive from life's adventures was not purely a conceptual one. Her feminism, her social and political beliefs, her passion for literatures of all cultures urged her to consider that life's adventures might include more than an attitude of the soul and its mood toward itself, the world, and God. Adventure may also indicate the *form* given to a life rather than a pattern discovered within it. Woolf investigates this possibility, as is her wont, first within the register of comedy, which emboldens as it enlarges her imagination, then more naturalistically, where, as an adventurer of the spirit, she must temporarily yield to the discouraging regime of social and sexual facts uncompromising.

Orlando, her comic romp in defiance of history, sexual custom, and narrative convention, is her supreme adventure. Never did Woolf feel so free to drop out of the continuity of life, range unchecked through time, work one miracle after another, includ-

ing, of course, the strangest departure from the regulated life of
nature and custom—Orlando's' transformation from a man into
a woman. The real perplexity for the fictional biographer and for
the reader of Orlando's life-adventure, however, is, if I may put
it this way, more lexical than gonadal. What should we call Orlando once he has departed from his former continuous male
identity and enters the unknown ways and customs of another
sex? Has the adventurer Orlando become an adventuress? Or has
he been transformed into a new species of being requiring a new
term—a female adventurer of the spirit perhaps?

Current and even traditional parlance suggest how deeply the
idea of adventure is compromised by the social fact of gender.
Webster's New World Dictionary dictionary notes, for example, that
adventuress as counterpart to the male adventurer is a rare
usage. The adventuress is generally understood to be "an un-
scrupulous woman who tries to become rich and socially accepted
by exploiting her charms, by scheming etc." That "scheming etc"
is parsed for Orlando—and for us—by those "poor creatures,"
Nell, Prue, Kitty, and Rose, who welcome Orlando into their exclusive, if fallen, society where they entertain her in a way that the
society of wits—Pope, Addison, and Lord Chesterfield—cannot
begin to equal:

> Each would tell the story of the adventures which had
> landed her in her present way of life. Several were the natural
> daughters of earls and one was a good deal nearer than
> she should have been to the King's person. None was
> too wretched or too poor but to have some ring or hand-
> kerchief in her pocket which stood her in lieu of ped-
> igree. So they would draw round the Punch bowl which
> Orlando made it her business to furnish generously, and

many were the fine tales they told and many the amusing observations they made for it cannot be denied that when women get together—but hist—they are always careful to see that the doors are shut and not a word of it gets into print.[14] (O, 160)

As amusing as the company and tales of these adventuresses may be, they contribute little to advance a modern sense of adventure. Their life adventures, which belong to the picaresque and parody its formulaic plots of upward mobility, are as negative as they are conventional, landing them, as they do at the end of the day, in a degraded position rather than in a morally or socially elevated state. This is not to be lamented, however, since Woolf's intention here is less to insinuate a new sense of adventure than to satirize an old one. Even that satiric target proves unstable, since she is less interested in revealing what adventures such women might have than in dramatizing how much pleasure they have in one another's company. It is not adventure, which isolates, but sociability, which unites, that these adventuresses have in common.

Let us determine, then, that Orlando is not an adventuress, but the harbinger of a social and human type new to modernity—the female adventurer. She is the modern woman whose sense of adventure extends beyond traditional categories of gender, but also beyond the conventional understanding of what an adventure might be. It is only as a woman, and then only after Orlando falls in love and marries—the stage in life when traditional women might feel that adventures of any kind should be behind and beyond them—that Orlando enters a state of mind that is markedly adventurous. Adultery is generally the only adventure the realist novel permits its married heroines. Adventure then becomes indistinguishable from transgression and reaps dire, merciless penalties. Orlando breaks with that tradition. In its first manifestation, her adventurous mind seems very much like the state of mind (as nurses call it) of the intemperate and deranged. "If one looks at the Serpentine in this state of mind," Orlando's biographer tells us,

> the waves soon become just as big as the waves on the Atlantic; the toy boats become indistinguishable from ocean liners. So Orlando mistook the toy boat for her husband's brig; and the wave she made with her toe for a mountain of water off Cape Horn; and as she watched the toy boat climb the ripple, she thought she saw Bonthrop's ship climb up and up a glassy wall; up and up it went, and a white crest with a thousand deaths in it arched over it, and through the thousand deaths it went and disappeared—"It's sunk," she cried out in an agony—and then, behold, there it was sailing again along safe and sound among the ducks on the other side of the Atlantic.
> "Ecstasy!" she cried. "Ecstasy!" (O, 210–11)

Lily's vision of the waters of annihilation pales before Orlando's wildly agitated vision of her husband caught in the sea surges of what appears to be, to Bonthrop's peril and our delight—a perfect storm! In her mind's eye, Orlando sees his ship climb a glass wall of water that will deliver him, along with a thousand other seafarers, to the abyss.

This vision of annihilation could reasonably be considered a sign of Orlando's mad perceptions had not her biographer earlier insisted that in such moments of visionary transport, "the thing one is looking at becomes, not itself, but another thing, which is bigger and much more important and yet remains the same thing" (O, 210). In other words, Orlando is not exhibiting signs of a deranged mind, but, on the contrary, of a highly imaginative one. She is, in fact, exploring the special powers of the adventurer as clairvoyant. For Simmel, the adventurer is the ahistorical individual disconnected from the past and having no continuous or predictable links to the future. Woolf adds to the inventory of social types the figure of the adventurer who is at once transhistorical and bipolar and so can occupy two positions in time and space, can be both herself and another, can voyage to the other side of the Atlantic while remaining stationed on the banks of the Serpentine. Reality, which for Woolf always means the irreducibility of things as things, is not violated—the boat remains the boat. But beyond and between things as they are, there is room to maneuver, to imagine things as they might be elsewhere, to venture beyond the bounds of the time and space continuum. The mind's destination, according to this visionary logic, is also its reward: "Ecstasy!" Ecstasy is the rapture that, like adventure, takes us out of ourselves ("ex-stasis"—stand out or apart) not as a dream, but as an exaltation. In such movements and at such ecstatic moments, Woolf fulfills her sense of adventure.

Woolf entertains a less ecstatic, more naturalistic, hence darker vision of life's adventure in *The Years*, a novel whose very title would seem to commit her to chronicling the uninterruptedness of existence. But in some ways the novel is her most poignant and revolutionary testament to the fictions of adventure. The novel begins by exploring the uncertain prospects for adventure through the hopeful route of childish fantasy, where its frailty as well as its charm is most exposed. "Now the adventure has begun" (Y, 27),

Rose Pargiter exults to herself as she prepares to steal from the safety of Abercorn Terrace, equipped with necessary provisions to last a fortnight. In this mood she is the brave ancestress of Maurice Sendak's wild things and ravagers of the night kitchen. With a child's genius for transforming the natural scene into a backdrop for imaginary adventure, she sets off to Lamley's with the same courageous spirits and high purpose as if she were, as she imagines she is, riding to the rescue of a besieged garrison. She surveys the street and determines that the coast is clear; she crouches close to the wall to escape detection, but when she reaches "the corner under the laburnum tree" she stands erect and then blurts out her adventurous identity: "I am Pargiter of Pargiter's Horse" (Y, 27). The dynastic hubris of family, class, and empire are transfigured in Rose's fantasy self, out of which a real adventurer might one day emerge.

This future is threatened when her spirited fantasy of conquest is challenged and finally routed by the sight of a man, his pock-marked face illumined and made more hideous by the flickering gaslight, sucking his lips in and out, mewing, unbuttoning his clothes. Adventure cannot survive this crass exposure to the brutish, fumbling naturalism of what Woolf, in *The Pargiters*, calls "street love, common love."[15] Rose is violently expelled from the landscape of adventure into an urban world where sexual barbarism rather than rebel insurgency is the enemy of civilized life. Still, I would insist that we should not overestimate the impact of this defeat, however lurid and traumatic the shadow it casts over the dreamscapes of adventure. The adventurous fantasy of being a leader of an expedition never deserts Rose and later becomes one of the consolations of her blighted life.

Nor does the affinity for adventure desert Woolf. Woolf's sense of adventure is vigorous and expansive enough to admit and survive its own defeat and disillusionment. In *A Room of One's Own*, Woolf worries that in representing her vision of *Life's Adventure* Mary Carmichael would be tempted to become "the less interesting branch of the species, the naturalist novelist, and not the contemplative."[16] For it is, of course, as the contemplative novelist, or, in the terms we have been developing, as an adventurer of the spirit, that Woolf at once realizes and defines her own modernity.

Even in *The Years*, her most naturalistic work, she seems less interested in documenting the barbarities and commending the civilities that make up the life of Monday and Tuesday than in exploring how, as Eleanor Pargiter phrases it in her moment of spiritual adventure, "we can improve ourselves . . . live more . . . live more naturally . . . better" (Y, 296). Eleanor, who will later be hailed as a "fine old prophetess" (Y, 328), is feeling at this moment "not only a new space of time, but new powers, something unknown within her." She is suddenly eager, despite her advancing age, for the supreme adventure—entering and exploring the new space of time, the new world she envisions: "When will this New World come? When shall we be free? When shall we live adventurously, wholly, not like cripples in a cave?" (Y, 297). Nicholas, her fellow adventurer and coconspirator in spirit, had groped for an image to give that adventurous feeling scope and direction: " 'The soul—the whole being . . . ,' He hollowed his hands as if to enclose a circle. 'It wishes to expand. To adventure, to form—new combinations?' " (Y, 296). Here Woolf's sense of adventure demands a new verb, as well as a new way, of being. Adventure is now promoted to the active form of a purposeful infinitive, in which, freed of the constraints of tense, person, or gender, it gestures outwardly, if indefinitely toward new spiritual horizons and possibilities. Who knows what new combinations of self and other, of the sexes, of mind and world, might emerge if the soul were to obey this summons to adventure?

In 1933 Alfred North Whitehead published his *Adventures of Ideas*, in which he proposed that any civilization, whatever its ideals and ideology, requires Beauty, Truth, Art, Peace, and Adventure.[17] No one, I suspect, would question that Beauty, Truth, Art, and Peace contribute to and define the essential ideals of any civilization, but many might wonder at the important role and place Whitehead accords to adventure. Yet for Whitehead, Adventure is the catalyst of these values, what keeps them fresh and vital presences. Adventure, he argued, was the spirit and the value that brought beauty, truth, art, and peace into being; it is Adventure that keeps beauty, truth art, and peace from decaying into stale or harsh orthodoxies. Civilization cannot rest on a platform of stability or be content with an achieved perfection. Civilization must advance or decline and decay. Adventure is the zest of the advancing world that keeps a culture from degenerating into staid convention. "New types of civilization are only possible," he argues, "when thought has run ahead of realization":

> The vigour of the race has then pushed forward into the adventure of imagination, so as to anticipate the physical adventures of exploration. The world dreams of things to come, and then in due season arouses itself to their realization. Indeed all physical adventure which is entered upon of set purpose involves an adventure of thought regarding things as yet unrealized. Before Columbus set sail for

America he had dreamt of the far east, and of the round world, and of the trackless ocean. Adventure rarely reaches its predetermined end. Columbus never reached China. But he discovered America.[18]

Woolf is the Columbus of the Human Inside. Adventure is for her both a state of mind and an infinitive, imperative verb by which she dares to imagine things as yet unrealized. As the novelist of life's adventures, she is always dreaming of new worlds, new spiritual and social combinations even as she charts the established and persisting world of the everyday. In her fictional and polemical writing, Woolf takes on the life and identity of realist, traditionalist, experimentalist, elegist, fantasist, psychologist, humorist, truth teller, social critic, dramatist, but if, as *Orlando* proposes, there is "the Captain self, the Key self, which amalgamates and controls them all" (O, 310), that Captain self that I would have us salute is Woolf the Adventurer.

Epilogue

8

Anon Once More

"Suddenly the sense of what people are leaves one. I return him to the pool where he will acquire lustre" (W, 244). Thus muses Bernard, in one of his abstracted moments in *The Waves* when the reality of the world or of other people seems to desert him. Abstracted, but, remarkably, not bereft, not even forlorn. He seems, indeed, admirably calm and deliberate in the face of this sudden loss. He seems intent on converting a passive sense of loss into a willing relinquishment of what he calls, with gentle mockery, "these minute objects which we call optimistically 'the characters of our friends.' " He consigns these characters to a pool, located, one supposes, deep in the recesses of the mind where their look, and perhaps even their value, will be enhanced.

Woolf plays nimbly on the verbal relation between pool and the historic root of luster—the *lustrum,* the Roman ceremony of purification of the people performed every five years after a census. The civic lustrum becomes a metaphor for the purification, but also the refreshment, of the demon of reading, indeed of the most difficult reading we routinely hazard, the reading of other people.

To acquire luster, the people we know should be returned to the pool where they will be cleansed of the common pollutants—familiarity, prejudice, the demons of hate, love, and countless other emotions that have adulterated their image over time. So, at least, Bernard's little fable of reading seems to advise.

Our sense of an author—what I have been calling the figment we conjure in the course of our reading—also benefits from such periodic lustrations. Without them, our relationship to writers is in danger of becoming dulled, even tarnished, by conventional and unfeeling responses. If we fail to heed the demon of reading that whispers I hate or I love, we can no longer expect to remain on intimate terms with the writers we read. Not only do words become unreal when we try to banish feeling from our reading, but, Woolf warns us, "we, too become unreal—specialists, word mongers, phrase finders, not readers." "In reading," Woolf advises, "we have to allow the sunken meanings to remain sunken, suggested not stated; lapsing and flowing into each other like reeds on the bed of a river."[1] How inviting is this image of the reader's mind as a pool or river in whose depths mere words, but also the authors who increase our sense of what words are and can do, acquire the luster that eventually might bring a new radiance to the world.

I have tried to follow Woolf's advice and resist becoming what my training had prepared me to be—a specialist, a wordmonger, a phrase finder. But it hasn't been easy to give myself over completely to the demon of reading. In this book I have taken pains to sort out what I learned from reading someone I know well—Virginia Woolf—in order to bring her artistic personalities into sharp, angled, mutlilayered, and (one always hopes) lustrous relief. Yet in the course of our long acquaintance, I found myself more, not less, confounded by evidence of her different personalities as they surface in her fiction, her diaries, her letters, her juvenilia, her reviews and essays, her literary and political tracts, and all the biographies and memoirs, not to mention all the literary criticism published in or for her name. I wanted to put all these selves in relation to one another, to compose, in my own mind, an image of what Huxley called, with how much irony it is not easy to decide, the Whole Personality.

I should, of course, have known better. After all, I knew from my experience both as a private reader and as a teacher that the relation between author and reader is a precarious and always partial one that reflects the mood of the writer while writing, but also the mood that motivates or overtakes the reader while reading. But now I appreciate this precariousness not as a problem, but as a possibility. This is the possibility that the demon of reading perpetually holds out to us. Woolf never lost her respect for this demon and

the diabolic power which words possess when they are not tapped out by a typewriter but come fresh from a human brain—the power that is to suggest the writer; his character, his appearance, his wife, his family, his house—even the cat on the hearthrug. Why words do this, how they do it, how to prevent them from doing it nobody knows. They do it without the writer's will; and often against his will. No writer presumably wishes to impose his own miserable character, his own private secrets upon the reader. But has any writer, who is not a typewriter, succeeding in being wholly impersonal? Always, inevitably, we know them as well as their books.[2]

So it is always and inevitably that readers come to know writers as well as their books. We know them without their consent and often against their will. Most important of all, we know them primarily and most intimately as figments that exist only in our imagination. This is the form, I have been arguing, that our knowledge of the author takes. It is a knowledge, I also have been arguing, that, however phantasmal and partial it may be, is as valuable as it is inevitable.

Nevertheless, there are still times when I lose a sense of what and who Virginia Woolf is, even though her sentences are as familiar and at times as dear to me as were the lines in my mother's face. She once again becomes for me Anon, a voice without a name, without a traceable face, a mere figment. In such circumstances, Woolf (or her figment) suggests I return her to the pool where she might acquire a new luster. Even as I do so, I wonder what fresh face she will present to me when she next emerges.

Notes

Chapter 1: The Figment of the Author

1. J. M. Coetzee, *Diary of a Bad Year* (New York: Viking, 2007), 132–33.

2. W. B. Yeats, "A General Introduction to My Work," in *Essays and Introductions* (New York: Collier Books, 1961), 509.

3. Virginia Woolf, "How Should One Read a Book?," in *Second Common Reader* (New York: Harcourt, Brace, 1960), 243.

4. Roland Barthes, *Sade, Fourier, Loyola,* tr. Richard Wilbur (New York: Hill and Wang, 1976), 8.

5. Quentin Bell, Woolf's nephew, wrote the first and still somewhat controversial biography, *Virginia Woolf: A Biography* (London: Hogarth, 1972). Each decade seems to call forth a renewed need to grapple with her relatively uneventful but fascinating existence. In sequence as they appeared: Lyndall Gordon, *Virginia Woolf: A Writer's Life* (New York: W. W. Norton, 1984); Hermione Lee, *Virginia Woolf: A Biography* (New

York: Knopf, 1996); Julia Briggs, *Virginia Woolf: An Inner Life* (New York: Harcourt, 2005).

6. Winifred Holtby, *Virginia Woolf: A Critical Memoir* (London: Wishart, 1932).

7. Terry Eagleton, "Buried in the Life: Thomas Hardy and the Limits of Biographies," *Harper's*, November 2007, 89.

8. Aldous Huxley, "Fashions in Love," in *Collected Essays* (New York: Bantam, 1963), 75–76.

CHAPTER 2: PERSONALITIES

1. Personalities in *The Moment and Other Essays* (New York: Harcourt Brace Jovanovich, 1974), 167.

2. "Indiscretions," in *The Essays of Virginia Woolf*, ed. Andrew McNeillie (San Diego: Harcourt Brace Jovanovich, 1988), 3:463–64.

3. Ibid., 461.

4. "Personalities," 171.

5. Ibid., 169.

6. Ibid., 169–70.

7. Virginia Woolf, *A Room of One's Own* (New York: Harcourt Brace, 1981), 73.

8. Ibid.

9. Ibid., 56.

10. "The note of banishment, banishment from the heart, banishment from home, sounds uninterruptedly from *The Two Gentleman of Verona* onward till Prospero breaks his staff, buries it certain fathoms in the earth and drowns his book. It doubles itself in the middle of his life, reflects itself in another, repeats itself, protasis, epitasis, catastasis, catastrophe. It repeats itself again when he is near the grave, when his married daughter Susan, chip of the old block , is accused of adultery. But it was the original sin that darkened his understanding, weakened

his will and left in him a strong inclination to evil." James Joyce, *Ulysses* (New York: Vintage, 1986), 174.

11. "Personalities," 169.

12. Ibid.

13. "Indiscretions," 461.

14. "Personalities," 170.

15. Ibid.

16. Lee, *Virginia Woolf,* 522.

17. Virginia Woolf, *Orlando* (New York: Harcourt Brace, 2006), 73. Future citations of this novel are noted as O in the text.

18. Virginia Woolf, "Montaigne," in *The Common Reader* (New York: Harcourt Brace Jovanovich, 2002), 68.

19. Ibid., 59.

20. Auerbach, *Mimesis* (Princeton: Princeton University Press, 1991), 290, 291.

21. Virginia Woolf, *To the Lighthouse* (New York: Harcourt Brace Jovanovich, 2005), 7. Future citations are noted as TTL in the text.

22. *A Room of One's Own,* 3.

23. Virginia Woolf, " 'Anon' and 'The Reader': Virginia Woolf's Last Essays," ed. Brenda R. Silver, *Twentieth-Century Literature* 25, no. 3/4 (Fall–Winter 1979), 382.

24. Virginia Woolf, "Reading," in *The Essays of Virginia Woolf,* 3:143. This historic theme is take up again in "Anon," where it is more fully elaborated: "The Elizabethans are silent. There is no little language nothing brief, intimate, colloquial. When they write the rhythm of the Bible is in their ears. It makes their speech unfamiliar. It is only expressive of certain emotions. Thus when Lady Ann Bacon writes to her son she is a preacher addressing a subordinate. Fear of God and distrust of man surround her as with the walls of a dungeon. She admonishes; she exhorts. The actual object—it is a basket of strawberries is approached circuitously ceremoniously. Greek and Latin come as easily to her pen

as a French phrase comes to ours. They [wrap themselves] about in a cumbrous garment when they [try] to talk." "Anon," 388–89.

25. "Notes for Reading at Random," in "Anon," 376.

26. "Reading," 155.

27. Ibid., 156.

28. Ibid.

29. Virginia Woolf, *The Diary of Virginia Woolf,* 5 vols., ed. Anne Olivier Bell and Andrew McNeillie (London: Hogarth Press, 1977–1984), 5:75.

30. *A Room of One's Own,* 99.

31. John Keats, "Letter to John Hamilton Reynolds, 3 May 1818," in *Romanticism: An Anthology,* ed. Duncan Wu (Oxford: Blackwell, 1998), 1021–22.

32. *The Diary of Virginia Woolf,* 2:13–14.

33. Virginia Woolf, "Letter to a Young Poet," in *Death of the Moth and Other Essays* (London: Hogarth Press, 1942), 142.

34. "Reading," 157.

35. Gordon Allport, *Becoming* (New Haven: Yale University Press, 1955), 18.

36. Ibid., 19.

37. These dispositions, Allport contends, are not a "matter of specific gene determination or of instinct, except perhaps in the broadest possible sense. I refer to certain latent or potential capacities that play a crucial role in becoming. Every young animal, for example, seems to have the *capacity to learn.* . . . If he is normally endowed the human infant will in time develop a conscience, a sense of self, and a hierarchal organization of traits. He will become some sort of structural system, self-regulating and self-maintaining. What is more, he will exert himself to become something more than a stencil copy of the species to which he belongs." Ibid., 26. Italics are Allport's.

38. Virginia Woolf, *The Waves* (San Diego: Harcourt Brace Jovanovich, 1959), 289. Future citations are noted as W in the text.

39. Virginia Woolf, *The Years* (New York: Harcourt Brace, 1967), 334. Future citations are noted as Y in the text.

40. Marcel Proust, *Swann's Way*, trans. Lydia Davis (New York: Penguin, 2002), 19.

41. Ibid., 20.

42. Virginia Woolf, "Street Haunting: A London Adventure," in *Death of the Moth*, 24.

43. Ibid.

44. Ibid., 27.

Chapter 3: The Sibyl of the Drawing Room

1. *The Letters of Virginia Woolf,* ed. Nigel Nicolson and Joanne Trautmann (New York: Harcourt Brace Jovanovich, 1978), 1:149.

2. There are many personal recollections and personal accounts of Bloomsbury. The most comprehensive critical history of the group is S. P. Rosenbaum, *Edwardian Bloomsbury,* 2 vols. (New York: Macmillan. 1994).

3. *Letters,* 1:119.

4. Ibid., 99.

5. Ibid., 147.

6. Virginia Woolf, "Old Bloomsbury," in *Moments of Being* (New York: Harcourt Brace Jovanovich, 1976), 170.

7. Virginia Woolf, "22 Hyde Park Gate," in *Moments of Being,* 144.

8. Thanks to Christine Froula for pointing out that George's pig eyes were as essential to Woolf as his dark crisp ringlets for understanding his nature.

9. "22 Hyde Park Gate," 144.

10. Ibid., 145.

11. Ibid., 155. When she recapitulates the last, abruptly scandalous pages of "22 Hyde Park Gate" at the opening of "Old Bloomsbury," Woolf recalls George's attentions this way: "It was long past midnight that I got into bed and sat reading a page of two of *Marius the Epicurean*

for which I had then a passion. There would be a tap at the door; the light would be turned out and George would fling himself on my bed, cuddling and kissing and otherwise embracing me in order, as he told Dr Savage later, to comfort me for the fatal illness of my father—who was dying three or four storeys lower down of cancer" ("Old Blooms-bury," 160). The entire question of George Duckworth's sexual "male-factions" is a complex and much disputed one, but for the most careful weighing as well as reading of the evidence, see Lee, *Virginia Woolf,* 147–56.

12. "22 Hyde Park Gate," 145.

13. Ibid., 142.

14. "Old Bloomsbury," 162.

15. "22 Hyde Park Gate," 142.

16. Ibid.

17. "Old Bloomsbury," 164.

18. Ibid., 169.

19. Ibid., 168.

20. Ibid.

21. Ibid., 166.

22. Virginia Woolf, "Phyllis and Rosamond," in *The Complete Shorter Fiction of Virginia Woolf,* ed. Susan Dick (San Diego: Harcourt, 1985), 18. Future page references are noted as SF in the text.

23. The phrase is Woolf's elegant shorthand for the ordinary life of an ordinary day with which, Woolf argues, the modern novel ought to concern itself. See Virginia Woolf, "Modern Fiction," in *The Common Reader: First Series,* ed. Andrew McNeillie (San Diego: Harcourt, Brace, Jovanovich, 1984), 149–50.

24. "Old Bloomsbury," 163. See especially Christine Froula, "Civili-zation and 'My Civilization': Virginia Woolf and the Bloomsbury Avant-Garde," in *Virginia Woolf and the Bloomsbury Avant-Garde: War, Civili-zation, Modernity* (New York: Columbia University Press, 2005), 1–34.

25. Virginia Woolf, "Memoirs of a Novelist," in *The Complete Shorter Fiction of Virginia Woolf,* 70. Future references are noted in the text.

26. Virginia Woolf, "The Value of Laughter," in *Essays of Virginia Woolf,* 1:59.

27. Ibid., 59.

28. "Tell me, Bart," Lucy Swithin asks her brother, "what's the origin of that? Touch wood. . . . Antaeus, didn't he touch earth?" In Virginia Woolf, *Between the Acts* (San Diego: Harcourt Brace, 1969), 25. Future citations are noted as BA in the text.

29. "The Value of Laughter," 60.

30. Virginia Woolf, *Night and Day* (New York: Oxford University Press, 1992), 15–16. Suzanne Raitt's excellent introduction helps place the novel within Woolf's own family lineage. See especially pp. xxv–xxvii. Julia Briggs offers a shrewd reading of *Night and Day* as a drawing room comedy whose courtship plot is "filtered through" Leonard Woolf's *The Wise Virgins,* a novel more forthright about issues of class and race. See Julia Briggs, *Virginia Woolf: The Inner Life* (London: Allen Lane, 2005), 29–35.

31. Virginia Woolf, *Mrs. Dalloway* (London: Penguin Books, 1992), 133–34.

32. "The Value of Laughter," 60.

Chapter 4: The Author

1. Woolf did not register herself since, as Hermione Lee notes, "she was in the dark cupboard of her mental illness, and did not emerge until the autumn of that year." But 1915 did see the publication, delayed by war, of her first major effort as an author, *The Voyage Out.* See Lee, *Virginia Woolf,* 322.

2. Virginia Woolf, "Craftsmanship," in *The Death of the Moth,* 126.

3. "Prose," she matter-of-factly admits in "The Narrow Bridge of Art," "has taken all the dirty work on to her own shoulders; has answered

letters, paid bills, written articles, made speeches, served the needs of businessmen, shopkeepers, lawyers, soldiers, peasants." See *Collected Essays,* ed. Leonard Woolf (London: Chatto and Windus, 1967), 3:223.

4. Of course, the *ideological* impact of her writing is undeniable, especially in such polemical works as *Three Guineas.* But Woolf never forges manifestoes, issues guidelines, or gives instructions that must be followed to the letter.

5. "Modern Fiction," 150.

6. The book being reviewed was J. D. Beresford's *An Imperfect Mother.* See *The Essays of Virginia Woolf,* 3:195–97.

7. See Hermione Lee's excellent discussion of Virginia Woolf and the language of madness in her *Virginia Woolf,* 187.

8. Samuel Beckett, *Murphy* (New York: Grove Press, 1957), 65.

9. James Joyce, *Ulysses,* 592.

10. Elaine Showalter insightfully remarks on how Woolf uses skywriting, a "brand-new phenomenon when Woolf was composing her novel," as a "cinematic linking device." See her "Introduction," in *Mrs. Dalloway,* xxiii–xxiv.

11. "On Being Ill," 11.

12. Auerbach, *Mimesis,* 532.

13. "Divisions of novelists into ventriloquists: soliloquists." "Notes for Reading at 'Random,' " 374.

14. Detachment, but not indifference. The one pose Woolf was never desirous of mastering was the godly impassivity that the aloof creator Stephen Dedalus holds up as a model for his own writerly aspirations, one that would mimic "the God of creation . . . invisible, refined out of existence, indifferent, paring his fingernails." James Joyce, *A Portrait of the Artist as a Young Man* (New York: Penguin World Classics, 1993), 233.

15. *A Room of One's Own,* 65.

16. *Diary,* 2:14.

17. Ibid., 5:135.

18. The word *humour* is freighted with associations for the English mind. In its original sense it denoted the various moistures of the body that accounted for the dominant types of human temperament—sanguine (blood), melancholy (black bile), phlegmatic (phlegm), choleric (choler). This sense survives in our speaking of someone as good or ill-humored, but for the literary-minded, Ben Jonson's "humour" characters, comic eccentrics whose inflexibility originates in moral as much as bodily imbalances, give a special piquancy to the phrase "odd humor."

19. Gillian Beer, "The Body of the People in Virginia Woolf," in *Women Reading Women's Writing,* ed. Sue Roe (Brighton: Harvester Press, 1987), 87.

20. Ibid.

21. "Modern Fiction," 150.

22. Virginia Woolf, *Pointz Hall,* ed. Mitchell A Leaska (New York: University Publications, 1983), 34.

23. Ibid., 61.

24. Virginia Woolf, *The Voyage Out* (Oxford: Oxford University Press, 1992), 249. Further citations are noted as VO in the text.

25. "A Sketch of the Past," in *Moments of Being,* 129.

26. *A Room of One's Own,* 87–88.

27. "A Sketch of the Past," 129.

CHAPTER 5: THE CRITIC

1. Woolf, "How It Strikes a Contemporary," in *Common Reader,* 234.

2. Woolf, "Coleridge as Critic," in *Essays,* 2:222–23.

3. "Indiscretions," 460.

4. Woolf, "Byron and Mr. Briggs," in *Essays,* 3:478. There is also an endearing portrait of a man of "pure and disinterested reading," whose character and motives differ completely from those of the man of learning, in "Hours in a Library," *Essays,* 2:55.

5. "Byron and Mr. Briggs," 482.

6. Woolf, "Lives of the Obscure," in *Common Reader*, 107.

7. Woolf, "Thomas Hood," in *Essays*, 1:159.

8. "Lives of the Obscure," 106.

9. "Coleridge as Critic," 223.

10. Woolf, "How Should One Read a Book?" in *Second Common Reader*, 234.

11. *Diary*, 4:145.

12. "How Should One Read a Book?" 246.

13. "Phases of Fiction," in *Collected Essays*, 2:56.

14. "Hazlitt," in *Second Common Reader*, 164.

15. "How It Strikes a Contemporary," 355.

16. "Coleridge as Critic," 222.

17. Her reign and death are described in Woolf, "Professions for Women," in *Death of the Moth*, 149 passim.

18. This hobgoblin appears at the very end of *A Room of One's Own* (114), as the incarnation of all that is oppressive and censorious in the regime of patriarchy.

19. Ibid., 39, 114.

20. Ibid., 49.

21. "How It Strikes a Contemporary," 355.

22. Woolf, "The Patron and the Crocus," in *Common Reader*, 206–7.

23. Woolf, with deadpan humor, suggests that there might be a way to negotiate "a union that is profitable, to the minds and purses of both" reviewers, of whom there are too many, and authors, who are so prickly. "It should not be," she maintains, "a difficult problem to solve. The medical profession has shown the way. With some differences the medical custom might be imitated—there are many resemblances between doctor and reviewer, between patient and author. Let the reviewers then abolish themselves or what relic remains of them, as reviewers, and resurrect themselves as doctors. Another name might be chosen—consultant, expositor or expounder; some credentials might be given, the books written rather than the examinations passed; and a list of those ready and authorized to practise made public." Virginia Woolf, "Reviewing," in

Captain's Death Bed (London: Hogarth Press, 1981), 127. Leonard Woolf defended the role of reviewers and literary journalism generally as a service to the reading public overwhelmed by the mass production of books. Woolf had already acknowledged the revolution in the economic organization of literature in "The Patron and the Crocus," although she still insisted that the reader and reviewer ought not to concern themselves with following and analyzing popular and commercial successes, but with becoming real patrons, creating a fit and demanding audience for writers. Looking back to the Elizabethan authors, writing for the aristocracy and the playhouse public, or, more recently, the nineteenth-century authors writing for "the half-crown magazines and the leisured classes," Woolf concluded that for the modern writer, the question of "audience" was less simple, and indeed constituted a "predicament." "The Patron and the Crocus," 206.

24. " 'Anon,' " 383.

25. Gertrude Stein, "What Is English Literature," in *Lectures in America* (London: Virago, 1988), 13.

26. Ibid.

27. "Reading," 142.

28. *A Room of One's Own*, 71.

29. Ibid., 72.

30. Woolf, "Hours in a Library," in *Essays*, 2:60.

31. Woolf, "Bad Writers," in *Essays*, 2:328.

32. "What Is English Literature," 17–18.

33. Woolf, "Middlebrow," in *Essays*, 2:196.

34. "A Sketch of the Past," 129.

35. Woolf, "On Not Knowing Greek," in *Common Reader*, 23.

36. The "in or about" retains just enough of the liberal spirit of approximation to indemnify the confident precision of December 1910. It is generally agreed that Woolf chose 1910 because that year saw the death of King Edward VII and the First Impressionist Exhibition, two events to mark a generational divide. Less commonly remarked, but a literary fact Woolf did not fail to note, is that 1910 saw the reissue and

double printing of Samuel Butler's *The Way of All Flesh,* a book Woolf considered to have paved the way for the modernist assault on repressive social conventions. It should finally be remarked that 1910 also saw the deaths of Mark Twain, William James, and Tolstoy, and the abolition of slavery in China. A new world was in the making, even as the old was in the throes of dying. The famous claim appears in "Mr. Bennett and Mrs. Brown," in *Captain's Death Bed,* 91.

37. "Modern Fiction," 150.

38. Woolf, "Notes on an Elizabethan Play," in *Common Reader,* 52.

39. "Modern Fiction," 150.

40. "Notes on an Elizabethan Play," 54.

41. " 'Anon,' " 383.

42. "The Reader," 428.

43. Woolf, "The Pastons and Chaucer," in *Common Reader,* 7.

44. Ibid., 9.

45. Ibid., 11.

46. Woolf, "The Elizabethan Lumber Room," in *Common Reader,* 45.

47. "Notes on an Elizabethan Play," 57.

48. Ibid.

49. "Montaigne," 58.

50. Ibid., 67.

51. "The Elizabethan Lumber Room," 47.

52. Woolf, "Jane Austen," in *Common Reader. Persuasion* suggests this likelihood, since its famous outburst on woman's constancy "proves not merely the biographical fact that Jane Austen had loved, but the aesthetic fact that she was no longer afraid to say so" (144).

53. These ideas are adumbrated most concisely in "Modern Fiction," "How It Strikes a Contemporary," "Mr. Bennett and Mrs. Brown," and "The Narrow Bridge or Art." These essays date to the 1920s, when modernist practices were establishing themselves as indispensable innovations that responded to the catastrophe of the Great War. By the 1930s the aesthetic principles of modernism were to be challenged by a new

generation of artists, who, seeing the conditions that led to the second great war of the century, began to question and often renounce the "spiritualism" of their immediate forebears and to rely on "materialist," politically and socially charged justifications for the work of art. Woolf's "The Leaning Tower" is among the most influential and important essays of the 1930s to address this issue, and *Three Guineas* is her most important tract expressing her views on the relationship between patriarchy and war, literature and politics.

54. *A Room of One's Own*, 76.

55. Woolf, "Women Novelists," in *Essays*, 2:314.

56. Woolf, "Men and Women," in *Essays*, 3:193.

57. *A Room of One's Own*, 98.

58. Ibid., 113.

CHAPTER 6: THE WORLD WRITER

1. I am grateful to Paulo Asso for his invaluable help in alerting me to the possible significance of Xenophila. His diligent research revealed the following: "In the 'Paulys Realencyclopädie der classischen Altertumswissenschaft' vol. IX A.2 [Munich, 1983] columns 1565–7, eight men named Xenophilos are listed. I could not find any Xenophila (or Xenophile, as the feminine would sound). As for the adjective 'xenophilos [xenpophile] xenophilon' (a form for each gender, m. f. and neut.), it sounds like a completely possible formation, but it is NEVER attested in the extant corpus of ancient Greek literature. Nor is it familiar to me from Modern Greek." E-mail correspondence from Paolo Asso, 12 October 2003.

2. Alex Zwedling's *Virginia Woolf and the Real World* (Berkeley: University of California Press, 1987) and Jane Marcus's *Virginia Woolf and the Languages of Patriarchy* (Bloomington: Indiana University Press, 1987) are pioneering works that brought needed attention to Woolf's worldly and public concerns. The most recent of their notable successors

include Rachel Bowlby's *Virginia Woolf: Feminist Destinations* (Oxford: Blackwell, 1988), Michael Tratner's *Modernism and Mass Politics* (Stanford: Stanford University Press, 1995), Melba Cuddy-Keane's *Virginia Woolf, the Intellectual, and the Public Sphere* (Cambridge: Cambridge University Press, 2003), Marcus's own, somewhat self-revisionist *Hearts of Darkness: White Women Write Race* (New Brunswick: Rutgers University Press, 2004), and Christina Froula's *Virginia Woolf and the Bloomsbury Avant-Garde.*

3. Stephen Spender, Obituary Notice, *Listener*, 10 April 1941, reprinted in *The Critical Heritage*, ed. Robin Majumdar and Allen McLaurin (London: Routledge and Kegan Paul, 1975), 426.

4. Malcolm Cowley, review of *Between the Acts*, *New Republic* 6 October 1941, 440, reprinted in *Critical Heritage*, 450.

5. Auerbach, *Mimesis*, 552.

6. Ibid.

7. "On Not Knowing Greek," 28.

8. Virginia Woolf, "The Russian Point of View," in *Common Reader*, 178, 180.

9. Virginia Woolf, "*The Cherry Orchard*," in *Essays*, 3:246.

10. Ibid.

11. "The Russian Point of View," 173.

12. "*The Cherry Orchard*," 247.

13. "On Not Knowing Greek," 23.

14. Ibid., 30.

15. This bar confronts us whenever we attempt to reach across cultures. It is not simply a question, as it is in large part with Greek drama, that we are separated by such a great historical divide and that we do not even know how the words the choruses are saying are pronounced. Russian literature, which is contemporaneous with our own, suffers a similar, if indeed not greater, degradation. We can no more easily pass into the Chekhovian delicacies or Dostoevskyean convulsions of the Russian soul than we can be transported into the ecstasies of the Greek

choruses. The Russians, too, suffer miserably in translation, a depriva-
tion Woolf regards as catastrophic. In translation, she vividly observes,
"the great Russian writers are like men deprived by an earthquake or a
railway accident not only of their clothes, but also of something subtler
and more important—their manners, the idiosyncrasies of their characters. What remains is, as the English have proved by the fanaticism of
their admiration, something very powerful and very impressive, but it is
difficult to feel sure, in view of the mutilations, how far we can trust
ourselves not to impute, to distort, to read into them an emphasis which
is false." "The Russian Point of View," 178.

16. Ibid., 175.

17. Virginia Woolf, "The Russian View," in *Essays*, 2:343.

18. "The Cherry Orchard," 248.

19. Auerbach, *Mimesis*, 552.

20. Virginia Woolf, *Three Guineas* (Oxford: Oxford University Press,
1992), 365.

21. "On Not Knowing Greek," 36.

22. Ibid., 31.

23. Ibid.

24. "Modern Fiction," 154.

25. "On Not Knowing Greek," 36–37.

26. Sigmund Freud, "Humour," in *The Standard Edition of the Complete Psychological Works of Sigmund Freud*, ed. James Strachey (London:
Hogarth Press, 1975), 21:162.

27. Ibid., 166.

28. "On Not Knowing Greek," 39.

29. "Humour," 163.

30. Mark Hussey suggested to me that Woolf's utopian version of
common cause and common nature might also have been registered in
Lily Briscoe's fantasy of emotionally attaining "the isle of blessed boots."

31. Asso, e-mail correspondence, 14 June 2003.

CHAPTER 7: THE ADVENTURER

1. For a study of more traditional fictions of adventure, see Paul Zweig, *The Adventurer* (New York: Basic Books, 1974), especially 3–18, 223–52.

2. *A Room of One's Own*, 80.

3. Ibid.

4. Roland Barthes, *A Lover's Discourse* (New York: Hill and Wang, 1979), 13. Zweig, in discussing the adventurer as a "poignant male fantasy," makes the more extreme claim that "The adventurer is in flight from women." See *The Adventurer*, 79, 61.

5. *A Room of One's Own*, 81.

6. Georg Simmel, "The Adventurer," in *On Individuality and Social Forms* (Chicago: University of Chicago Press, 1971), 187–88.

7. *Letters*, 1:212.

8. Simmel, "The Adventurer," 188.

9. Eudora Welty, "Foreword," in *To the Lighthouse* (New York: Harcourt Brace Jovanovich, 1981), xi.

10. Plunge, of course, is the energetic, fateful word that launches her first great modern narrative of inward voyaging, *Mrs. Dalloway*: "What a lark! What a plunge!" (MD, 3).

11. A clear and resonant echo of the inner terrain where Mrs. Ramsay's adventures as a wedge-shaped core of darkness take her.

12. Simmel, "The Adventurer," 192.

13. Ibid., 194.

14. Anne Fernald offers a compelling and indeed adventurous reading of this scene as "a reminder of the topics that remain taboo and a fantasy of what society might be like if women were accepted as full participants" in the public sphere. See her "A Feminist Public Sphere? Virginia Woolf's Revisions of the Eighteenth Century," *Feminist Studies* 31, no. 1 (Spring 2005): 176–77.

15. Virginia Woolf, *The Pargiters* (New York: Harcourt Brace Jova-novich, 1978), 50.

16. *A Room of One's Own*, 88.

17. Alfred North Whitehead, *Adventures of Ideas* (New York: New American Library, 1956), 273.

18. Ibid., 278.

CHAPTER 8: ANON ONCE MORE

1. "Craftsmanship," 129.

2. Ibid.

Index